Praise for Eleanor Roosevelt's *It's Up to the Women*

"Eight decades after the Great Depression, American women are facing yet another test of courage and ingenuity. Eleanor Roosevelt's advice to women living through the world's greatest economic crisis remains relevant, comforting, and, for all of its practicality, profoundly inspiring."

—AMANDA FOREMAN, bestselling author of *Georgiana* and *A World on Fire*

"In 1933, Eleanor Roosvelt launched her first book to galvanize an urgent movement for democracy, peace and freedom. As fascism threatened the world, she believed women's activism would save the future. IT'S UP TO THE WOMEN, she argued, to educate healthy, socially engaged children who would preserve nature and prevent the extinction of 'whole species.' ER cautioned against desertification: 'If one cuts down all the trees . . . the water supply will be dried up. . . . One does not destroy what nature gives us to love and conserve.' This book, bold & vividly written, is needed NOW!"

—BLANCHE WIESEN COOK, Distinguished Professor of history at John Jay College, author of a prize-winning three-volume biography of Eleanor Roosevelt

"Grounded in the concerns of America in the Great Depression, Eleanor Roosevelt's *It's Up to the Women* was relevant then, and it is relevant now. It challenges women anew to foster community, adhere to the highest standards of ethics, raise fearless children with a concern for the world, and embrace and act on the notion that it is 'the attitude of women towards changes in society (that) is going to determine to a great extent our future in this country.' Steeped in a narrative and the vocabulary of another time, this treasure of a book reminds us that: the fight is not over for an income that is secure and sufficient to raise a family; we have yet to fully respect and value the work of those who care for others; and the most important role in a democracy is that of the citizen. Inspiration for the work ahead on the challenges of the 21st century is found here, in wise advice for women in the 1930s."

—JULIA STASCH, President, John D. and
Catherine T. MacArthur Foundation

"This must-read primer by America's greatest First Lady is so much more than quaint, decades-old history. It powerfully reminds us of how much women have achieved since Eleanor's time—and how much more must be done to secure the level playing field she advocated. Ably re-introduced by the brilliant Jill Lepore, this book is as timely now as when it first appeared in the depths of the Depression. What Eleanor advised women then remains truer than ever today: our mission will only be fulfilled when 'we can say we never saw a wrong without trying to right it.'"

—JENNIFER J. RAAB, President, Hunter College
and founder of Roosevelt House at Hunter

IT'S UP TO THE WOMEN

IT'S UP TO THE
WOMEN

ELEANOR
ROOSEVELT

Introduction by

JILL LEPORE

NATION
BOOKS
New York

Published by Nation Books, an imprint of Perseus Books, LLC, a subsidiary of Hachette Book Group, Inc.
116 East 16th Street, 8th Floor
New York, NY 10003

Nation Books is a co-publishing venture of the Nation Institute and Perseus Books

Books published by Nation Books are available at special discounts for bulk purchases in the United States by corporations, institutions, and other organizations. For more information, please contact the Special Markets Department at Perseus Books, 2300 Chestnut Street, Suite 200, Philadelphia, PA 19103, or call (800) 810-4145, ext. 5000, or e-mail special.markets@perseusbooks.com.

Designed by Jeff Williams

Library of Congress Control Number: 2017933155
ISBN: 978-1-56858-594-9 (HC)
ISBN: 978-1-56858-595-6 (EB)

10 9 8 7 6 5 4 3 2 1

CONTENTS

CONTENTS

INTRODUCTION

Jill Lepore

In the fall of 1932, when Eleanor Roosevelt was teaching American history at a high school for girls, editing a magazine called *Babies—Just Babies*, and helping her husband in the last weeks of his run for president of the United States by making a gazillion campaign stops—a speech here, a photograph there—the Associated Press assigned a political reporter named Lorena Hickok to follow her around. "She is, to use the expression of one of her friends," Hickok wrote, "a whirlwind." Roosevelt wore "ten dollar dresses," refused the protection of the Secret Service, borrowed friends' cars so she could drive herself, and on Sundays scrambled the eggs herself, at the table, in a chafing dish. "THE DAME HAS ENORMOUS DIGNITY," Hickok telegrammed the AP one day. "SHE'S A PERSON."

That November, Franklin Delano Roosevelt won forty-two out of forty-eight states in one of the most lopsided elections in American history. His wife celebrated, but she was a reluctant first lady. "Eleanor Roosevelt was a new phenomenon in America politics," writes Blanche Wiesen Cook, Eleanor's most exhaustive biographer. Born in New York in 1884, Eleanor Roosevelt was orphaned as a child. She married in 1905; FDR was her fifth cousin. The marriage was an unhappy one. In 1914, while ER was raising the couple's six children, FDR began a passionate affair with his social secretary. Eleanor wanted a divorce; Franklin believed a divorce would ruin his career. They stayed together. She began regularly speaking in public in 1921, after he was struck with polio and she appeared in his stead. By the 1920s, she'd become a major figure in Democratic politics, just at a time when women were entering political parties. In 1920, with the ratification of the Nineteenth Amendment, the National American Women's Suffrage Association reinvented itself as the League of Women Voters. "The only way to get things in this country is to find them on the inside of the political party," said Carrie Chapman Catt. Roosevelt took that advice to heart, becoming a leader of the Women's Division of the

New York State Democratic Party while her husband campaigned and served as governor of the state. By 1928, she was head of the Women's Division of the Democratic National Committee.

Eleanor Roosevelt never wanted her husband to run for president. When he won, she told friends she might divorce him rather than lose her independence to the honorific role of first lady. "I shall have to work out my own salvation," she said. She decided to reinvent the role. What should a "first lady" really do? Not host parties, she thought. She went on a national tour to crusade on behalf of women. She wrote a regular newspaper column. She became a champion of women's rights and of civil rights (in support of racial equality, she was the most outspoken member of her husband's administration). And she decided to write a book. She called it *It's Up to the Women.* She announced her plan in January 1933, two months before her husband's inauguration. "Mrs. Franklin D. Roosevelt, who has been one of the most active women in the country since her husband was elected President, is going to write a 40,000-word book between now and the March inauguration," the *Boston Globe* announced. "Every word will be written by Mrs. Roosevelt herself."

To say that Roosevelt's act of writing this book was shocking hardly covers it. In 1933, women rarely spoke in public, held very few public offices, and had barely begun voting. During one of FDR's reelection campaigns, supporters of his opponent wore buttons that read, "We Don't Want Eleanor Either." And yet her own supporters were legion. In September 1933, reporter Rita S. Halle watched Eleanor Roosevelt at a conference about how to help the needy through the winter. The first lady told a story about an evicted family sleeping in a house with no windows against the rain, and the baby had gotten sick and died. Halle wrote of ER: "Despite a lithe, graceful figure, she is not beautiful. She does not charm by her personal appearance. Yet, as she spoke, the wearied audience uncurved its collective spine until, all over the large room, men and women were sitting forward on their chairs in intent response to the magnetism of her simple sincerity."

That's a fair account of *It's Up to the Women*, too, with its earnest charm and flinty steadiness. In giving advice about getting through hard times, Roosevelt called on her study of the past. "There have been other great crises in our country and I think if we read our history carefully, we will find that the success of our nation in meeting them was very largely due to the women in those trying times," she wrote. The *Hartford Courant* called it, accurately enough, "a book of general counsel and advice on pretty well everything, from dish-washing to high diplomacy." In chapters on everything from what to cook for dinner to how to make a family budget (spend no more than 38 percent on food and 25 percent on rent), Roosevelt urged women to care for their children and their husbands but not to stint on taking care of business and thinking about politics. Vote, and get a job if you can, she told women. As for children who complain about their mothers working outside the home, and, equally, for husbands who might complain about their wives: "They have a right to expect that if they have a problem she will listen to it, but they have no right to expect that she will give up that which she loves and which is constructive and creative work, because they would like to have her home at five o'clock instead of at six o'clock." The "really new deal for the people," Roosevelt said, had to do with women awakening "to their civic duties."

Reviews of the book ranged from politely dismissive to politely outraged. In a column titled "Mrs. Roosevelt's Book," the *Christian Science Monitor* called it "a wholesome, pleasant, kindly effort." "Mrs. Roosevelt has always been an independent thinker," the *Chicago Tribune* averred. "Her typewriter has developed no inhibitions since its journey to the White House."

It's Up to the Women was the first book Eleanor Roosevelt wrote. It would not be the last. She hammered at that typewriter, year after year, telling the story of her life and urging women to enter politics for decades before, at the end of her public life, she chaired JFK's Commission on the Status of Women. "Can a woman ever be president of the United States?" she asked in an essay published in *Cosmopolitan* in 1935. Not soon, she thought. But someday. Meanwhile, there's no end of important work to be done, by everyone.

JILL LEPORE is the Kemper Professor of American History at Harvard and a staff writer at the *New Yorker*.

IT'S UP TO THE WOMEN

FOREWORD

THE title of this book will suggest the thought which I have in mind in writing it—namely, that we are going through a great crisis in this country and that the women have a big part to play if we are coming through it successfully.

There have been other great crises in our country and I think if we read our history carefully, we will find that the success of our nation in meeting them was very largely due to the women in those trying times. Upon them fell a far heavier burden and responsibility than any of us realize.

Undoubtedly, for instance, the women who landed from the *Mayflower* faced in that first winter in the stern

New England country the first great crisis in the development of our nation. When we look through the old houses still standing and learn from contemporary documents and letters of the conditions under which the Pilgrims of New England lived and the part they played in conquering starvation and the wilderness, we will give to the Pilgrim mothers at least as much credit as to the Pilgrim fathers. What those hardships meant, how bitter and desperate they were, we have only to look at the inscriptions on the monument at Plymouth, naming those who died that first terrible winter, to realize. This was a real battle in which many women and children paid with their lives for their heroism. I think it is equally true that the Revolution itself would never have been won unless women had been able to bear the hardships and privations, and carry on the work of their homes while the men fought for freedom.

And in that later crisis, of the war between the states, we get a vivid picture in a short story by Dorothy Canfield* of how it was "up to the women" to carry on while

---

* In "Hillsboro People," Henry Holt & Co.

the men were fighting at the front. The description of a woman who farmed the land, planted the garden, got in the hay and tended the stock while her husband fought to free the slaves and preserve the Union, is made particularly poignant by her answer when asked what she did when she heard her husband was killed at Gettysburg, "I went on hoein' my beans. But I ain't mindin' tellin' you that I can't look at a bean-row since, without gettin' sick to my stomach!"

The women know that life must go on and that the needs of life must be met and it is their courage and their determination which, time and again, have pulled us through worse crises than the present one. The present crisis is different from all the others but it is, after all, a kind of warfare against an intangible enemy of want and depression rather than a physical foe. And I hold it equally true that in this present crisis it is going to be the women who will tip the scales and bring us safely out of it.

Many of us are afraid because we have lost pleasant things which we have always had, but the women who came over in the *Mayflower* did not have them, neither did the women who farmed in the uplands of Vermont during the Civil War. Perhaps we need again a little of the stern stuff our ancestors were made of. In any case, it will do us no harm to look at ourselves somewhat critically in relation to some of the problems that confront us to-day.

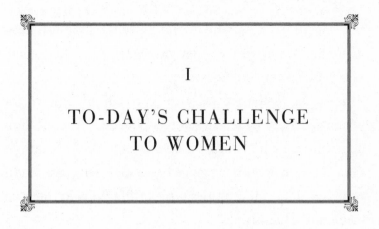

I

TO-DAY'S CHALLENGE
TO WOMEN

PRACTICALLY every woman, whether she is rich or poor, is facing to-day a reduction in income. Sometimes I think the most troubled people I know are the very rich, especially many of them who have grown up in idle luxury. They have never known what it was to deny themselves anything that they really wanted, and now they have to learn to do it cheerfully and without a feeling of martyrdom. Their fathers and husbands have always been able to give them, not only what they needed, but many pleasant things which seemed necessary to those who had really nothing to do, and who therefore felt they must have many luxuries in order to provide variety in what would otherwise be very dull existences.

It is not really necessary to go to the mountains for winter sports, or to seek a summer climate in the south in mid-winter, or in summer a comfortably cool climate in some far-away mountain range or on some sea coast, but if you have done these things all your life, to give them up seems a real hardship.

If a maid has always answered a bell when you rang it, if you have never sewed except to give your idle hands some occupation, it is somewhat disconcerting to find that you have to wait on yourself and that your sewing must serve some useful purpose such as mending a frock or darning your stockings.

I have a theory that the people who have had a great deal and who have the right kind of stuff in them, are the ones who most readily adjust themselves to doing without certain material things. This theory, however, only holds good where the people have had sometime in their lives an opportunity to live simply so that they have made the discovery that the luxuries of life are not really essential to happiness. These women who have lived in this luxurious fashion, and who do not have back of them at least the traditions of early ancestors who had education and some appreciation of the value of mental qualities, and yet who disciplined themselves and were inured to hardships, are frightened to-day and are making their husbands and fathers feel that because they have lost the ability to give them as much materially, they have ceased to be successful. Sometimes they do not even seem to realize that the men are as bewildered and as lost as they are. The men have likewise grown dependent upon their pleasures, perhaps not quite to the same extent, but still it is a rude change for them also. They, too, have gauged their success by how much money they could make. Therefore between such husbands and wives there arises the specter of failure.

Sometimes I think these are the most pathetic people in the world. Even love is an uncertain satisfaction with them, for to grow, love must really give.

When giving is too easy or is purely a matter of giving material things, it ceases to bring real happiness. Writers have often tried to show in poetry and in books how hollow was the relationship which existed between people where wealth had become so great that they depended largely on paid service and very little on each other for comforts or pleasures. The family has been pictured over and over again as gradually drifting apart and this theme is prominent to-day in the literature of every land.

Two people must really do things for each other and when things are done entirely by paid attendants, love is very apt to fade out of the relationship. The only thing that remains is the satisfaction of their mutual comfort, and that is not much foundation for happiness just now since they realize that any day they may lose all these comforts and pleasures. They have nothing more permanent to fall back upon.

All this is made doubly difficult because these women, never having learned how to work, are suddenly faced with the fact that they have no idea of how to take care of themselves. The mere thought that their husbands' earning power is cut down and may vanish entirely and their heretofore assured income may melt into thin air, fills them with apprehension. Instead of being helpful, the woman's own unhappiness and fear makes her add to the man's fears, thereby leaving the man less capable of meeting his difficulties.

I know one woman who, when she found her husband had used poor judgment and had done unwise things, started in on a campaign to make him realize how extremely wrong he had been not to consult her before he had made these mistakes. She talked to all their friends and they agreed with her that he had made mistakes, which many of them had made and which most men in these times had made, but she would only tell him how right they thought her judgment was and how very wrong, therefore, his judgment had been. The result was that the household grew daily more and more unhappy until finally even the little children realized that their father was in some way playing an inadequate rôle. This did no one any good and certainly did not help the man to recover his own self-confidence, and use better judgment, nor did it really help the woman to forget her losses and disappointments.

Another woman I know happens to be more or less alone in the world. She had been left a fair-sized fortune and found it extremely easy not only to live a life of luxury, but because she had wide interests and sympathies, she used her fortune to help many other people. She took the advice of others as to her investments and when hard times came she found that many of these investments sank to rather low levels, but she realized that her advisors had done their best. She did not berate them, she simply curtailed her own pleasures and luxuries in order to continue what she had been doing for other people, and she worked all the harder for certain things which she had started to develop herself, and which had been looked upon as unprofitable hobbies. To such good purpose did she work on these hobbies that they became her main source of income and they have enabled her so far to stand the strain of other losses. Hers is a spirit which would never blame other people and pull them down because she for a time had to face unusual hardships.

These women of wealth, however, will always be, on the whole, a small group and they certainly do not represent the larger group of our countrymen.

Leaving aside in this discussion the very present and distressing question of unemployment, most of the women in the country are women who are living on moderate-sized incomes, mostly earned, with few investments to take into consideration beyond perhaps the ownership of a small house or apartment. These women, many of them, have worked and most of them are willing to work again if they can get work. On the whole they are less afraid, though with each wage cut they have to make changes in their way of living and changes which do vitally affect their entire lives. It may not mean actually less food, but it does mean cheaper food. It means less help if they are accustomed to a maid; it means fewer movies; and if they have a car, it means fewer Sunday trips. It means endless little economies and constant anxiety for fear of some catastrophe such as accident or illness which may completely swamp the family budget.

Fundamentally we see repeated here on a larger scale many of the things we found in richer homes. The happy home will be the one in which the woman is not considering that her husband's success is measured by his salary. As long as the families are free from actual want, if the women can realize that happiness lies within and not without, if they can manage to recreate enjoyment in some of the simpler pleasures which our thriftier ancestors in other countries enjoyed, and which they brought with them to this country; if they can learn to make it a game to get the most out of their dollars and above all to spend their money for those things which they really want, then they will have real success.

It seems to me that we do not really give much thought to what we want out of life, and the development of this thought is one of the things which we can get out of the present depression. We should be able to realize that making up our minds as to what gives us the greatest amount of pleasure and then working for it, is one of the satisfactions of life. Drifting along is easy to do but if we want to see a real pattern in our lives, we must take the trouble to sit down and think out not only what we want for ourselves but what we want for our families. In the past when we did this our wants were chiefly for material things, bigger and better houses, more entertainment, more food, better clothes, etc. Perhaps in the future we may think up some new wants which will not cost more money but which will cost a little more effort. It might be well if we thought a little about doing things which would develop in our children new resources and interests in life. I am often struck by the fact that the members of our younger generation, whether they are rich or poor, feel that to have a good time they must go out and spend money. When life was simpler and there was less money to spend, youth stayed at home and made its own diversions. They found interests in themselves and in their surroundings, which now they haven't time to develop. It may be a happy day for us when an evening at home is not considered wasted, but is looked upon as an opportunity for developing a hobby or cultivating a friendship.

I consider one of the most successful women I have ever met, a woman who was left a widow with five children, four girls and a baby boy a little over a year old. All she had in the world was a rather delightful roomy old house, near a nice old country village, with a mountain at the back and a meadow all around it, and a Carnegie pension of less than one hundred dollars a month.

She took her children to the old house. They attended the village school, and she served on the school board. Her school must have been a fairly good one, for her children all won scholarships at two of the best colleges in the country. They worked their way through. They brought their friends home for week-ends and they had more friends and more fun in a simple way than many of the rich boys and girls in their class. And yet she never had a maid. She and her children did all the work on the place. There were always plenty of books and plenty of good plain food, but very little else. All her children are fine characters and to me she is the outstanding example of what real success in life means.

Of course, the real advantage in having little money is that families draw closer together; they have to depend upon each other and they have to do things for and with each other and the result is that the clan spirit grows. I am sure that that spirit is an essential thing to foster in this country just as much as in Scotland.

A family which clings together can become a great force, not only in a community but in a country. We have seen it over and over again in our early days. The Adamses stand out in New England as being an essential part in the making of the traditions of their State. One individual Adams would amount to very little, but all of them together carried weight and much influence.

I think it is well, of course, to keep oneself from being blind to the faults of the members of one's own family, but it seems to be an almost universal trait that while families may be clear-sighted about each other, and may even criticize each other when they are alone, if any one else takes this liberty the whole clan will rise in defense of the attacked member. Perhaps this is not a good thing and yet I think there is a germ of strength in it and a lesson for all of us. It is better to look for what is good and try to praise. On the whole it is more stimulating. Answering the natural urge to defend the other members of the clan is the realization that by recognizing good qualities we strengthen them; by clinging together a family finally may become a powerful force.

Of course, when we come to the very poor homes it is more than ever up to the women; for the men, when they have work, have very little leisure and the women must work hard to keep their families decently clothed, clean and fed. The poorer we are the more education we really need; and yet, of course, the poorer we are the less education we usually have, so poor people will often struggle blindly against conditions which they have no way of controlling. I take off my hat to the courage of the many women in the tenement houses who, in spite of conditions which we would look upon as hopeless, manage to bring up their children, give them a desire to make something better of themselves, and keep before their eyes the fact that they are striving for a higher standard.

There is no less courage shown by women who live on farms or in villages, because while we have been apt to think that poverty bore down harder upon those in our cities, there is unquestionably much hardship in both villages and farm houses and the heroic fight of many women, particularly on isolated farms where they feel the lack of sustaining company, will go down as one of the fine things which has often been overlooked.

So many women are inarticulate, especially when they live in rural districts where they have little opportunity of mixing with other women. The city woman can sit on her stoop of a summer's night and chat with many neighbors. The country woman may live not so far away from a neighbor, but her daily round of toil is so exhausting that even the effort of a short walk is more than she can face at the end of her daily work. She often carries heavy anxieties for the health of her children without daring to call in a doctor because of the expense entailed. Many things are more difficult to obtain in rural districts than in our big cities and I hope very much that when we are considering how to improve the life on the farm we will give some very special thought to the life of the women and children, which on the whole is harder than that of the men.

In the first place the farm woman has very little opportunity for earning any money which she can call exclusively her own and this makes her entirely dependent on her husband. Also her opportunities for getting into town and seeing and doing things are much more limited. She has living creatures that have to be cared for and therefore cannot leave for very long periods of time.

I think the way in which farm women are tied down is well illustrated by the story of a friend of mine who was extremely interested in a building which was going up some ten minutes' walk from her farm house. I asked her one day why she did not go and see it and her response was, "I haven't been outside of my yard in nine months except to take the children to the doctor." It is not only the exhaustion of having many tasks but it is the fact that those tasks are never ending and that they demand her presence practically all of the time.

The farm woman does nowadays often have a radio, and more papers and letters find their way into farm homes than in the old days, but we have not given nearly as much thought to the proper recreation for young people and women on farms as we have to the recreation of young people and women who live in crowded city districts. Nor have we given as much thought to the health of people in the country. We take it for granted that people living in the country are nearer to the food supplies and do not require the effort of education which has been put into teaching city mothers how to feed and care for their babies and for themselves. And yet there is really less opportunity on isolated farms to learn from each other and you will often find the farmer sending all the milk to town and feeding his children on condensed milk, sending the vegetables to the market or grocer and keeping none for the children. He will buy certain foods for the cattle but rarely puts the same amount of thought into what he should feed his own family, with the result that there is much undernourishment in the country districts and oftentimes many serious physical defects which go undiscovered and uncared for because they do not have the advantage of the health agencies to call upon which the children in the city districts have.

Much more should be done in education for our rural children. We have worked out very little in the way of special courses and curriculum for them and yet there is real preparation for rural life needed, which should be started in all the schools from the time they are small children, not only to minister to their health and usefulness but to the enjoyment of their lives in the country.

Out of all of this that we are going through will perhaps come to us the realization that we have to develop ourselves to the maximum of our ability and our natural endowments. This may be difficult for we have become so accustomed to depending on outside things for our happiness that we have almost forgotten to delve within ourselves and find qualities and abilities which could make life for ourselves and those around us happier. Any one to-day, who is not actually in want and whose family, from no matter what source, has sufficient to live on, must realize that the task we have in hand is the building of a person, an individual who can rise above material circumstances and make himself face life and adversity manfully. If he does this, he is worthy of the respect and affection of those around him. If temporarily, a man should have to live on the earnings of the woman, there are many ways in which he can make life easier for her, and if instead of complaining and sighing over his own luck, he bestirs himself to fulfill in every way whatever work lies to his hand, he will be a big person and when the opportunity again presents itself for him, and his earning power returns, he will have earned the love and affection of his wife and children for what he has done as an individual at home.

On the other hand, the woman whose husband is placed in this position must be sure to appreciate the fundamental fineness that is required for a man to meet a situation of this kind adequately. She must be big enough on her part to realize the individual contribution that is being made, and to give it the proper appreciation. She can make life miserable or happy by her recognition of what are the important things in life. If she fails to realize that the development of qualities which will allow the man to make himself useful and important to his wife and children is a great achievement, then she will have failed to learn one of the lessons which these times can teach, and she will not have developed an appreciation of what self-development along many lines may eventually mean to the individual.

In every one of these groups the women, the wives and mothers are the inspiration of the homes, the persons for whom the men really work. They have it in their power to make life gracious and pleasant, or by bickering and nagging to make it an ugly thing. No one who does this with life can claim any real success, but whatever her income may be, whatever her fears may be, if she will try to control herself, and meet life, as far as material things go, with high courage and a light touch, she will hold her family together and have a more successful husband.

And, above all, that which both men and women must realize is that now is the time to prove that what is really important is the fundamental character of the individual and the personality. A man may be a success as a husband and a father, a neighbor and a citizen, even if his earning power at the moment has shrunk to almost nil. Just now frequently we are brought up against the fact that what a man can earn has no relation whatsoever to his capacity or his worth as an individual, but we ought to realize as never before, that if a man or a woman can face the present situation with cheerfulness and fulfill obligations in the daily contacts of life, he or she is really showing an amount of fortitude which should make us respect and admire the character which makes it possible.

In these times we cannot measure with the usual yardstick of material success, as we have done in the past. We must readjust our sense of values and only as we do this can we adequately help other human beings.

II

THE PROBLEMS
OF THE YOUNG MARRIED

YOUNG married people are probably having the greatest difficulty meeting the situations of to-day because they are having to adjust themselves to each other, which in itself is a difficult task, and at the same time they are obliged to meet the constant shifting of material conditions. They do not know from day to day what they will have to live on. I have in mind a young couple with two children who up to a month ago, were living on a scale of $4,000 to $5,000 a year. The man had a position and all was going well. Suddenly he lost his position. The girl has an income of

$1,200 a year which is so far fairly well assured. She is re-adjusting her life to the scale of $100 a month and he is starting to try to build up a business of his own, such as he was in before he was with the big company. This is not an easy task and requires from both of them an immense amount of tolerance and of unselfishness, and an under-standing of the problem which each of them is facing. This cannot be achieved without a struggle.

It is safe to say that the great majority of people to-day are living on incomes of from $1,200 to $2,000 a year. All are put to it to adjust themselves to the changes which re-quire character and courage, but more than any other group, young married people have the heaviest load, not only of making these material adjustments which every one is obliged to make to a certain degree at present, but of making all the adjustments which are always part of the first years of married life.

As I said in the last chapter, one of the things which will make the situation easier is an understanding of what they both want out of life. I think it is well for all of us to take stock at present and decide what are the ways in which we spend money which mean something tangible to our happiness. No one can really decide that for us because to some people certain things mean more than to others. I should be most unhappy if I could not buy new books, but having beefsteak for dinner would mean nothing to me whatsoever! And, so it goes with many of the expenditures of everyday life.

If a woman is young, pretty clothes mean a lot to her, but while it is doubtless most important for the older woman to be scrupulously neat and if possible, becomingly dressed, she will probably not be as interested in clothes for their own sake as the younger woman.

In one respect a revolution has been going on in this country, and I think it is going to spread more and more. We are coming to count largely on modern inventions, which simplify the work of running a home, and very little on anybody else's manual labor outside the family group. I think where it can possibly be managed one maid is a great boon even to a family of very moderate income, but the fact that more and more young women must of necessity care for their own children is something which I consider of great value to both the children and the parents.

If a woman does her own work, the vital thing for her to do is to organize it so well that when her husband returns home she is not an exhausted human being, but can still meet him with a smile and enter into whatever interests he may wish to discuss with her.

If she has a domestic helper in her household, she must remember that she is dealing with a human being, and it is well for her to try everything herself before she lays down her rules for any one else. I have a theory that, under our modern system in which it is rare for any one to have more than one maid in the house, if a young woman will systematize her own work, she can greatly assist whoever is working for her. For instance, if when she gets up she immediately puts her bedclothes to air, it will save either her or her maid the necessity of coming up to do it later on, or of making up the bed without airing. Habits of neatness can be formed by the mistress so that she keeps her own part of the house tidy, and when she enters the kitchen to give an order, or to do some piece of work, she does not leave behind her a trail of work for somebody else to do. Then the household will run smoothly, the maid will come to her for advice and she will soon find if she does her own part of the work, that there is no shirking on the part of those who work with her.

It is always better for people working in an office or in the home to work with you and not for you. In this matter of the household, whatever your circumstances may be, organize according to the special circumstances which are yours, face the facts no matter how disagreeable they may be, cut your cloth according to what you have, decide first very carefully what you want out of your home life, and then insist on achieving it.

Many people, however, feel that this change in domestic employment has had something to do with the unemployment situation for the girls and older women alike. A great many people feel that for middle-aged and older women this field of domestic activity is one which may very profitably be developed. I should agree heartily if we could put this occupation of domestic service on the plane of any other professional or industrial occupation. If hours, wages and conditions could be better regulated, and if the housewives could be trained as well as the maids, then I should feel that into many average homes might come great help and comfort for mothers, and into many a woman's life the possibility of new interest and occupation when her usefulness in more strenuous work has come to an end.

It seems to me that many a woman needs help in her home far more when she is young and newly married, and the comfort would be great of having a middle-aged woman, who has been through many of the difficulties which she is now facing, coming in to help her, but as a rule the expense entailed in this country makes it impossible. First of all to find people who are willing to take part-time work of this kind is difficult and the price it is possible for a young married couple to pay is very often inadequate.

My mail is filled with pleas from middle-aged and old women who feel themselves dependent on their children and yet would be so grateful if they could earn something, even a small amount, to pay something for their board and have a little spending money of their own.

I am sure people of this kind can be found in every community and if they would fit themselves they could be really useful for a few hours a day, either going in the afternoon to help get dinner or to stay on with the young children while the father and mother go out, or coming in the morning on busy days to do some of the washing or some of the cooking.

This would fill, in many communities, a real need for two different kinds of people, the young married and the elderly women. Of course, I feel that the stigma can only be taken from domestic service if it can be looked upon as a profession. The person undertaking it should do her work exactly as though she were going into a factory and be on a business footing, should expect no social recognition, no particular consideration, but simply go in and work her time and do what is expected of her, looking for no recognition other than the consideration which would be given to any worker who was doing her work well.

This requires, of course, on the part of the employer, training so that she may know how to handle her work and plan so that she can tell some one coming in to help her, just what there is to do and run it as she would run a business. This will put domestic service on its proper footing and will at least make part-time work something accessible to the middle-aged woman in the community.

The price for this work should be regulated by the prevailing living cost and by the amount generally paid for the particular type of work, taking into consideration, of course, any special responsibility assumed by the worker. As it is not work involving very heavy strain either physical or mental, as a rule the pay should be kept at a medium level.

Both part-time and full-time domestic employment should be undertaken by skilled workers under regular rules and employer and employee should agree to abide by them. The wages for both should be paid in the same way, taking into account the age and skill of the worker.

Many young married people spend more thought on show than on real comfort or on having what will make the family living and the relationship with friends happier and easier. This comes partly from the fact that in the past few years we have felt the stamp of success to be material possessions and therefore we did not set ourselves so much to living congenial lives as to accumulating as much money as possible in order that we might shortly have the same material possessions that some of our neighbors had. This conception of living is something which in older civilizations is not so apt to be the ideal of the mass of the people. England is dotted over with small country homes where people live in comfort very congenial lives with very little money. The same can be said of France. There one may find countless little villas, countless little apartments in small towns where people are content to live the kind of lives that they enjoy with the independence which I think we will some day emulate when we realize that, after all, life is lived from day to day.

When we admit that one can not retrace one's steps and live life over again, we may accept the fact that we might as well savor it and enjoy it as we go along and not always be striving for something in the future which after all we may never achieve nor enjoy.

Into every household, very soon after it becomes a household, there enters the question of society and so it seems fitting for us to inquire where and what is society? There was a time when it meant a little group of people, set apart from the rest, fortunate people who had not only money but through some accident of birth or of circumstance, were thrown with those whose word and action carried weight in the community and who were the people looked up to and copied by the rest of their fellow men.

But this kind of society has more or less ceased to exist. People "in society" to-day are the people of great wealth, or the people who manage to appear in newspapers frequently as being associated with people of great wealth. One's grandparents may have belonged to the best blood of America, who fought and bled for freedom in their different generations, but that will not give one recognition to-day in society if one is penniless or even has to be careful of one's expenditures. Society in this sense is of little importance to-day but society in the larger sense which means that human beings need contact with each other, and must have opportunities for knowing each other and for being mutually helpful, is growing more and more important.

There are still some inhibitions about society which make it a little difficult for certain people whose material resources are slight, to feel free to gather friends around them, and yet the best society is achieved where congenial minds and temperaments meet together and exchange and enjoy each other's thoughts. This costs nothing and may be achieved in the simplest of surroundings.

I think all young couples should start in as soon as possible to mingle with congenial neighbors and establish a society of their own. They should not be deterred from enjoying the society of those around them simply because they cannot give the same type of party which is given by their neighbors. I have had as good a time in the studio of a young and struggling artist where crackers and cheese formed the sole refreshments of the evening as I have ever had in the ballroom of the richest New York hostess.

One must set one's own standards of what one wants in society. One must not be too much influenced by others and above all one must not attempt to strive to match what somebody else is doing. "Keeping up with the Joneses" is no longer so important because Mr. and Mrs. Jones are apt not to be very sure how long they can continue doing what they have always done. It is becoming increasingly evident that what one *has* matters little; what one *is* means that one can gather around oneself those who wish to see real people without regard to anything except enjoyable relationships and real personality.

This kind of society is, of course, easier for older people to achieve. I remember very well in my youth certain agonizing moments when I felt that something had gone wrong with my domestic arrangements and I was thereafter branded as a poor and inadequate housekeeper. Then one day an older woman said a rather flippant thing which gave me quite a different point of view. She remarked that all the world loved a poor housekeeper because they could always pat themselves on the back and think how much better they did everything! If you are feeling sensitive and have perpetrated some social *faux pas*, just remember this little saying of an older woman and realize that after all it is the atmosphere of the party and the people we meet, and not what we eat or how it is served, that really matters. One of the best hostesses I know cooks and serves her own dinners, but she is always unruffled and if anything goes wrong, she takes it as a joke and so things rarely seem wrong to her guests.

Older people should be able to give to younger people a sense of values and make them realize what really matters and what does not matter in social relations, and one of the great benefits which should come to us with advancing years is the realization that after all anything we really want to do can be accomplished.

One may have to exert a little more energy than usual; one may have to take a little more responsibility alone than one wished to take; but if one really wants something, our elders should show us that it can be accomplished with comparative ease and that our dread of meeting some new situation is really a fear left over from our childhood when everything new we tried was an unknown adventure until we had accomplished it.

Society to-day means the big society of all men and women and each one of us in our own little sphere may have real society if we cultivate making friends and drawing around us congenial people. The more kinds of people we know, the more interesting will our lives be. And the younger we discover this and bring up our children in an atmosphere of friendliness and to a habit of understanding and congeniality with varied interests and conditions in life, the more vital will be our homes and the better a training place for the children whom we must eventually shove out of the nest.

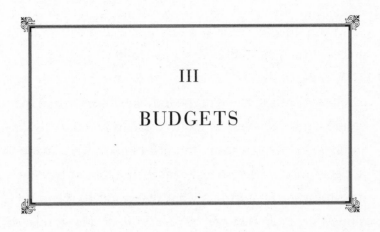

III

BUDGETS

FOR young and old in the present depression, we have discovered that budgets are necessary. We have to make a plan as long as we have a limited amount to cover our needs and we not only have to make a plan but we have to adhere to it. There is no use making a budget if we proceed to do as one young lady of my acquaintance did. Finding a number of attractive frocks that she considered "just too cute to give up," she far exceeded her budget and had to ask her husband to make up the deficit! This is not living up to the budget and a budget is of no use unless you live up to it.

In this chapter we deal a little more in detail with the practical carrying out of our desires in life.

A budget should be made up comprehensively and carefully to fit the needs of the individual person and individual family, as every one's needs are different. It is very valuable for many reasons, for, first of all in the making of it, people are obliged to make up their minds as to what is important to them in life; what they want to spend their money for. Then they will be obliged to decide on relative values and certain things which they need. Keeping to a budget is one of the best tests of character that I know of. It requires sometimes self-denial, sometimes discipline of a very strict variety, for there seem to be many reasons why exceptions should be made here and there. If you have never kept a budget, I advise you to do so and to stick to it not only for the satisfaction of knowing how your money is being spent, and why it has been spent, but also for the very distinct gain in self-control which will come to you as a result of your efforts. I am giving here certain simple rules for the making of a budget which may be helpful suggestions in the making of your own. These ideas have been suggested by experts and you may find them valuable in starting you off. In the end, of course, you will find yourself better fitted to make a budget for your own individual purposes.

The first thing for the young couple to do is to sit down together and list the necessities which enter into almost every one's daily life—rent (house operation, repairs, up-keep, improvements, etc.), heat, food, clothes, recreation, savings, insurance, doctors, miscellaneous.

There are prepared budgets which tell you the "proper percentage" of the income which should be spent for most of these items but these are very little use without consid-erable adaptation to the individual family.

After a study of several thousand families of average means was made, 38 per cent of the income was found to be the usual amount spent on food in the average family, but this, of course, did not mean that that percentage would be right for every family. In some families there would be fewer children and a different type of food would be supplied, and a man and his wife alone without young people needing special diets could often spend a very much smaller amount on their food. Food has come down in price generally so that at present the cost is lower and therefore the percentage spent out of the family budget for food should naturally be lower than when the price of food was high. When prices for food go up it may be necessary to spend a greater percentage of the family income on this item and this is one of the reasons that budgets have to be readjusted to individual needs and the variations in prices of different items.

The average amount spent for rent is 25 per cent of the total income. It is obvious therefore that it is necessary to know as nearly as possible what the total income will be to cover all the expenses of the family. Having determined what this may be, then find out what 25 per cent is and see if it is possible to get adequate living facilities for that price. It may be better to spend more on rent and less on food, particularly as the children get older, because they like to have a home where they can bring their young friends and not always feel that they are boring their elders.

There are certain social implications in your decision of how much rent you will have to pay. In considering rent you must also consider transportation for whatever wage earners are going to live in the house. If it is a young married couple, usually only one of them will have to go back and forth daily to work, but if it is a family with grow-ing children several members of the family may have to take daily trips back and forth to school or to work and the cost of their transportation may make it wise to pay more rent and live nearer their places of employment. This again is an individual question which each family will have to work out for itself.

One of the difficulties of growing girls is that they sometimes dislike staying with their elders and unless we find a way by which we can let them stay at home in comparative peace and quiet, they will go out with their young friends and we will be without any knowledge of what they may be doing. Hence the importance of living quarters.

In considering the family food expenses and in preparing menus, it would be well to go over Miss Flora Rose's menus or any menus prepared by a home economics college and see if it is possible to buy one's supplies more economically and have a nourishing and balanced diet at lower cost. Then consult cook books and newspaper suggestions in order to provide more variety. Miss Rose's menus are arranged to meet the limited incomes under which people are operating at present, and some of them are given in Chapter V.

Next comes the consideration of the item—"house maintenance," which includes such repairs as the home owner, even though handy with tools, cannot do himself.

These things seem small but usually mount up surprisingly, but this cannot be computed accurately. It must be decided by experience how much will be needed for heat, light, and telephone, which now forms a fixed charge in almost every type of house except those of the very poor and some farms in the country.

If a family owns its own home, then instead of rental they should compute all the expenses—taxes, interest on the mortgage, insurance, maintenance and repairs, as these are practically fixed charges and amount to the same thing as rent.

When you come to the third item, clothes, there is almost nothing that can be put down in a general way, for every family has special needs. I have found it very valuable always to make a clothes budget and to find out how long certain things which are expensive at the start can be worn. For instance, for me it pays to buy a rather expensive tailored suit, made to order, as I am not a size for whom it is easy to buy ready-made things, and I wear it a long time. I also happen to be very fond of hand work of all kinds and therefore hand-made underclothes have always appealed to me and I would rather put more money on underclothes and less on outer garments.

Here again the individual taste comes into play and therefore, while I would advise every woman to sit down and make a list of the clothes which she needs every year, to try on all of last year's things so as to ascertain whether they will still be sufficiently in fashion to keep her from being conspicuous in wearing them, one cannot lay down any hard and fast rule. One can usually count on a coat lasting two seasons, but a new hat will frequently make people think that everything one has on is new.

Clothes which the manual laborer needs are quite different from the clothes which the white collar worker needs and this also must be taken into consideration in making up the budget.

Do not think, however, that the price which you pay for clothes means a well-dressed or a poorly dressed woman. A ten-dollar dress, if you have good taste, may be just as pretty as one for which you have spent ten times as much. I have seen women who spend very small amounts on their clothes but who plan them carefully, frequently look better-dressed than women who waste a great deal of money and buy foolishly and without good taste.

The price of a garment is not always indicative of its real worth nor is it indicative of whether you are buying something that has been made under sweat shop conditions or not. This is a phase which even the poorest, in planning a clothes budget, should consider, for no matter what we can afford to buy, we cannot afford to buy at the expense of the health and strength of our fellow human beings. When you budget for your clothes remember to find out where you can buy economically but safely for your own health as well as for that of the workers.

To almost every one nowadays the owning of an automobile is a necessity and of course if you do own an automobile you must put that down as a separate item in your budget and be sure to include in the expense of a car the license, the insurance, the garage rent, repairs, and tires, as well as gas, oil and any other items of expense such as big repairs on worn-out machinery or eventual replacement of the car. These are all essentials in running the expenditures on a car successfully.

As to savings, the amount, even though it means the future of an old couple, cannot be estimated beforehand. It may be necessary for the family to spend every penny of income in order to give the growing children a chance to be really equipped for life and if this is the case, the older members of the family may have a very difficult time in saving any money at all and they may have to rely on being supported in their old age. This should be done, if necessary, with as little hardship to them as possible.

Also the unexpected expenses which arise in any family often take the accumulated savings of several years, such as illness, births, deaths, etc. It is safe as a rule in a normally healthy family to put down very little for doctors' bills, but a liberal allowance in young families must go for recreation. Nowadays we have reached a point in this country where nearly all young people look upon the spending of money as absolutely necessary in order to enjoy themselves. Therefore, it is time probably that we called a halt and made a study of the ways in which we can enjoy ourselves at a minimum price.

For instance, a holiday taken on foot or bicycle is far less expensive than a holiday taken in an automobile. England has kept to the bicycle, and most of her people at one time or another take walking, bicycling or camping trips. These camping trips frequently take the form of a small moving caravan drawn by a horse or donkey. If they go on bicycles, they enjoy all the obscure small places which are never reached by automobile.

We might well make it a game to discover what are the available places for holiday purposes where we can spend the least possible money.

Quite aside from our holiday, much money is spent in recreation such as movies and going out to dance places, particularly for young people, and I think while now and then these things are good, if we could get them to turn to some of the simple home things, such as an evening of games or of home music or of reading aloud, we might find ourselves spending less money and getting more real pleasure and profit for the family.

"Miscellaneous" will always be an awkward column, for so many things fall under the head which we haven't itemized in any way and which recur at varying intervals.

When everything has been estimated as nearly as one can, and you have cut down on all the things which you do not feel are absolute essentials, and finally the two sides of the ledger balance, then stop worrying about anything except the fact that you must try to live within your budget. And when you have added up what has gone in and what will probably have to come out, you may find that you are obliged to eliminate whole sections which you had thought indispensable in your budget, but this has had to

be done from time immemorial and I imagine every generation can go on finding this budget-making a thrilling
experience!

I started my budget when I was married and kept it reli-
giously until my conscience would allow me to keep my
accounts in my check book, but when my daughter married I gave her the same books which I had had and they
served as a guide for her first budget. However, she found
that she had many things which were different from my
needs twenty years earlier, and her budget and that of my
son showed very little resemblance to my own old one.

As I look back upon it, wages were but a small part of
my budget, but we know now that any family on the level
where they can afford to employ help of any kind, has a
very different wage to pay from that which we paid twenty
years or twenty-five years ago.

The same thing holds good of most of the things we
buy or do, but even though you may find it difficult, you
will find it interesting to keep an account of your expenditures from month to month, and be able to compare them
for several years. Only in this way will you ever be able to
make up your mind where your money has gone and how
many items you can cut out of your expenses.

A budget is a necessary evil no matter how dull you may find it, and it is equally necessary for the woman with an income of fifteen dollars a week as for the woman of unlimited means.

The material for this budget planning was furnished by Miss Flora Rose, College of Home Economics, Cornell University, Ithaca, New York.

IV

BUDGETING YOUR TIME

WE have had a chapter on budgeting our incomes, but at the present time it seems to me that the budgeting of our time is almost as important.

As I watch some of my friends toiling through their days, I realize how important it is to plan one's work and even plan one's leisure. Of course, different circumstances make for different types of activity, but whether one lives on a farm or in a village or in a big city, whether one's income in cash is practically nil, or runs up into the thousands, the necessity for planning is always there. I would like to consider for a few minutes the way this can be done in various types of households.

The woman on the farm starts her day very early. If she has several children, she should train them as soon as possible to be of some assistance. This will be more trouble to her at the start, but they gain greater efficiency as time goes on. If she has an old house, she is forced to take a great many more steps than she would in a modern house but if she takes advantage of the extension courses carried on by the state college of agriculture in practically every state, she is fairly sure to find that the home economics department will help her to arrange her kitchen and her house generally so as to require as few steps as possible. They will also advise her as to the type of furnishings to buy, things which will be strong and sturdy and yet not too costly. They will show her the best methods of mending and doing over old things that she may have and will help her with the beautifying of her home and at the same time show her how to get things which can be kept clean easily.

An effort should be made to get through the heavy work by one or one-thirty o'clock every day. Of course, emergencies arise but I am talking about the regular daily routine. A couple of hours' rest should be allowed for before the regular afternoon work has to begin. If you live on a dairy farm the work is more constant and it is harder to get away, but one way or another, a half day's holiday or an evening of entertainment should be planned once a week.

Do not get into the habit of feeling that you can never leave home. If you live in a community where the farms are far apart and you have to take your children with you, take them with you but if you possibly can, try to come to some agreement in the community whereby you combine with your neighbor now and then to take her children and let her take yours when you want to have a day or an evening or only a half day of freedom. It is a rare person who can get on without some break in the regular routine. Budgeting time to arrange for these breaks is just as important as it is to plan the income. Sometimes you may want to go to some civic meeting or church meeting in your afternoon free time and if you have a child old enough to leave in charge this is quite simple, but if not there may be in the neighborhood some older girl who will be willing to come and relieve you in return for some favor which you may be able to do for her. Rest does not mean sitting with your hands folded. If you need extra sleep, perhaps you can get a nap, but if not, sewing or reading or doing some kind of work you enjoy may be your rest. It simply means that your regular routine work should be off your mind.

I have often found with children, though it may seem like a foolish thing, that if you can get them in the habit of dressing in a certain way every day, they will get through very much more quickly, and I think this holds good in all kinds of regular work. For instance, if a child is trained to get up and wash and brush her teeth and then to put on her clothes without stopping to do other things in between and she has been told when she gets out of her bed to pull it apart and air it so that when she is finished dressing she can make it up, it will be a great help to the mother and to the child when she grows up. This need not be only the girl's job; there is no reason in the world why a boy should not learn to put his bedclothes to air even if he does not have to make the bed. If the room is tidied before she leaves it, or before he leaves it, it will take much less time for any actual cleaning that may have to be done.

I cite this as an example of the way one can conserve time by planning even such a little thing as how one gets up in the morning and prepares for the beginning of the day.

Many women start their breakfast cooking before they finish dressing, but if it is all part of the regular routine, one will get through much more quickly than if one does it differently each day.

You may say that you do not have to do any work in your household and therefore budgeting is not so important to you, but if you have any desire to be of real use in the world, you will find that there are many things which you could do and which you should do if you are not tied down by the actual physical care of your home and therefore, if you plan on getting up and seeing your husband off for business and your children off for school and giving the necessary directions to your household, you will have that much more free time for civic and charitable occupations and for doing the numerous little kindnesses to friends and neighbors which mean so much in community life. The greatest benefit which money can bring to any of us is freedom of mind, so that we may think of things which will lighten the burdens of others and a freedom of time in which to do some of these things. The less you are tied down by the care of your home and the care of your children, the greater your obligations to plan your time intelligently. If you are a woman alone in the world and even freer to do as you wish, then you will find that only through interest in work of some kind, which will require budgeting your time, will you get any lasting satisfaction in life. I think it is a fallacy that the things which we buy or the things which we may do purely for our own pleasure because we are free of responsibilities and cares, bring us joy. In the end the only lasting pleasure comes from the joy of sharing something with some one else and seeing their pleasure. The more you budget your time, the more you can do, and the more happiness of this kind will be yours.

But if you budget your time for work, you must budget your time for play as that is essential for every one. Above all remember that your health must be intelligently safe-guarded, for no human being can neglect watching his own health conditions and budgeting your time will require arranging for enough sleep, enough time to eat without too much hurry and enough time for outdoor air and exercise. This is most important for the women who live in a town or for the women free from the necessity of physical work in their own homes. Housework is exercise and is frequently done or should be done with the windows wide open, but if you work with your head, or indoors a great deal, this particular part of the budget is very important. Your physical condition rests on your mental condition and on your spiritual attitude toward life. A nervous and irritable person can do little to make life pleasant for those around her; therefore it is up to us to study our physical needs well and to budget our lives to meet these requirements. I am not unmindful that there are many people whose lives are so filled with toil that even budgeting seems hopeless, but we are entering, many of us I hope, into new social conditions in which there will be more leisure even for the woman who works in a factory or shop and has a home to keep as well. And so budgeting becomes even more necessary than it has been in the past. It was hopeless to try to plan a day which included ten or twelve hours in a mill and in the remaining hours one was obliged to sleep, eat and care for the children and keep the home, but under new social conditions there may not be any twenty-four hours of this kind and it makes budgeting not only more necessary but more helpful. We will realize from day to day that new hopes of many kinds may be fulfilled if all of us work intelligently toward the creation of a new kind of social world that is just beginning to dawn on us as a possibility.

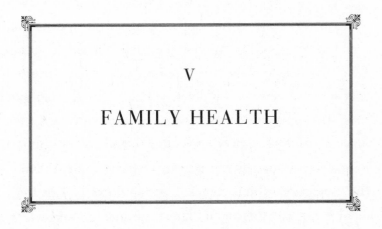

V

FAMILY HEALTH

FAMILY health is something to which we must all give attention, for on our physical condition depends so much the happiness of family life. We all realize that the physical and mental are very closely bound together and that the old saying, "Mens sana in corpore sano" (A sound mind in a sound body) has always been true and has never been truer than in this present-day situation when the outside world has changed so much, and we find ourselves constantly adjusting to new physical conditions, and hurtling through space at a constantly increasing rate of speed.

For every normal human being fresh air is essential. Our forefathers thought that the night air would surely bring malaria or some dire disease, but we have learned that if we screen our windows and keep out the mosquitoes, the night air does no harm. So sleep with open windows, consult a doctor when feeling ill and do not wait too long, exercise enough so that you keep the ability to enjoy the recreation which comes from rapid exercise in fresh air. Do not eat too much. There are many books which tell what foods are considered to contain the necessary fats and proteins and vitamines. Balanced diets can be obtained from a physician but if one does not wish to worry to this extent, I think many of the same results can be achieved from eating with moderation.

For many, as they grow older, a very light breakfast, one good substantial meal a day with either a light lunch or a light supper will make for both mental and physical fitness. It is commonly said that people dig their graves with their teeth and I think that it is fairly true in many cases. It is also wise to eat slowly and if possible with some congenial companion. A book will do if no human being is at hand!

Too much emphasis cannot be laid on the importance of the preparation of food and the choice of food where the family health is concerned.

Children can eat a great deal and still be undernourished and the adults in the family also may eat and not get the maximum amount of good out of their food, so the mother of a family should look upon her housekeeping and the planning of meals as a scientific occupation. At the present time there is so much less money to be spent on food in most families, it is fairly important that the mother study all the latest suggestions in the way of inexpensive and yet nourishing meals.

I am putting in here a sample week's menus and recipes prepared for the Temporary Emergency Relief Administration by the New York State College of Home Economics at Cornell University. These recipes will serve a family of six. Many of these meals we have used ourselves at the White House. They have been worked out under the direction of experts on home economics and will serve as a sample for balanced, inexpensive home rations.

MONDAY

Breakfast

Farina-Milk-Sugar, Whole Wheat Toast-Butter, Milk for Children, Coffee for Adults.

Dinner

Meat Loaf-Creamed Potatoes, Lettuce Salad, Whole Wheat Bread-Butter, Stewed Prunes, Milk for Children.

Supper

Scalloped Tomatoes with Cheese, Whole Wheat Bread-Butter, Scotch Wafers, Cocoa for All. Give only weak cocoa to young children.

MEAT LOAF: (Can be made into meat balls and cooked on top of stove.) 1 pound ground beef, 1 cup bread crumbs, 1½ teaspoons salt, 1 medium onion, minced. Milk or water, pepper. Mix all the ingredients together, thoroughly, adding enough milk or water to moisten well. Bake in a moderate oven about 1 hour.

SCALLOPED TOMATOES: Canned or fresh tomatoes, salt and pepper, grated cheese, few drops onion juice, sugar, buttered bread crumbs.

If canned tomatoes are used, drain off some of tomato liquid and save for breakfast. Season tomatoes with salt, pepper, onion juice, and sugar if liked sweet. Cover bottom of buttered baking dish with crumbs, cover with tomatoes, cover with a layer of cheese and sprinkle top thickly with crumbs. Bake in a moderate oven (375 deg. Fahr.) until crumbs are brown.

SCOTCH WAFERS: 2 cups rolled oats, 1 cup sifted flour, ½ cup sugar, ½ teaspoon salt, 2 teaspoons baking powder, 3 tablespoons fat, ⅓ cup milk.

Mix the dry ingredients, add the fat and mix together thoroughly. Add enough milk to make a dough sufficiently hard to roll (about ⅓ cup). Knead this dough well. Roll very thin, cut with a biscuit cutter. Bake in a moderately hot oven (375 deg. Fahr.) for 15 to 20 minutes. When cool the wafers should be very crisp.

TUESDAY

Breakfast

Oatmeal-Milk-Sugar, Whole Wheat Toast-Butter, Milk for Children, Coffee for Adults.

Dinner

Hot Stuffed Eggs-Tomato Sauce, Mashed Potatoes, Whole Wheat Bread-Butter, Prune Pudding, Milk for Children.

Supper

Apple and Cabbage Salad, Peanut Butter Sandwiches, Cocoa for All.

For the two- or three-year-old child the tender leaves of cabbage may be chopped and put in a sandwich.

HOT STUFFED EGGS: 5 eggs, hard cooked; ½ teaspoon minced onion, 1 teaspoon vinegar or tomato juice, ¼ teaspoon salt, pinch of pepper.

Cut the eggs in half lengthwise, removing the yolks. Mash the yolks thoroughly, mix with other ingredients. Stuff the egg whites. Put in a dish, cover with tomato sauce, reheat in a slow oven and serve. A white sauce may be used instead of tomato sauce.

TOMATO SAUCE: 1 cup tomatoes, ¼ cup water, 1 teaspoon sugar, 1 tablespoon fat, 2 tablespoons flour, ¼ small onion, chopped fine, ½ teaspoon salt. Cook tomatoes, onion, sugar, water and salt together for five minutes. Rub through a coarse sieve. Melt fat, add flour and blend thoroughly. Add tomato mixture slowly, stirring constantly. Cook until it thickens.

Note: For a white sauce use milk instead of the tomato mixture.

PRUNE PUDDING: ¼ pound prunes, 1½ cups cold water, ½ cup sugar, 2 cups prune water, 1 inch stick cinnamon or ¼ teaspoon powdered cinnamon, 4 tablespoons flour, 4 tablespoons cold water.

Soak the prunes overnight in the 1½ cups cold water. Cook in the same water until they are tender. Drain, but save the liquid. Remove the seeds and cut prunes into bits. Add sugar, cinnamon and hot prune juice. If juice does not measure 2 cups add enough water to make up the measure. Bring to the boiling point and simmer for 10 minutes. To the flour add the 4 tablespoons cold water and mix to a smooth paste. Add this slowly to the prune mixture, stirring carefully, and cook for 10 minutes over a slow fire or over boiling water. Remove stick cinnamon (if used) and pour into bowl or a mold. Serve cold.

COCOA: 2 to 3 tablespoons cocoa, 2 cups cold water, few grains salt, 3 cups fresh or diluted evaporated milk, 2 or 3 tablespoons sugar, few drops vanilla, if desired.

Combine cocoa, sugar, salt. Mix well and add cold water. Boil 5 to 10 minutes. Add the scalded milk and heat. Beat a few seconds with an egg beater or a spoon. Add vanilla if desired and serve. For the two- to three-year-old child add 2 tablespoons of the cocoa prepared for the rest of the family to his cup of warm milk.

WEDNESDAY

Breakfast

Tomato Juice for Children, Oatmeal-Milk, Bread-Butter, Milk for Children, Coffee for Adults.

Dinner

Vegetable Stew, Whole Wheat Bread-Butter, Caramel Blanc Mange, Milk for Children.

Supper

Scalloped Potatoes with Milk, Carrot Relish, Whole Wheat Bread-Butter, Tea for Adults, Milk for Children.

VEGETABLE STEW: 1½ cups dried lima, navy, kidney beans or lentils, 2 quarts cold water, ½ cup rice, 2 cups tomatoes, 1 onion, 4 tablespoons drippings.

Wash and soak the beans overnight in water. Drain and add fresh water to cover well. Boil for three hours. Brown sliced onion in frying pan, with drippings; add this to the cooked beans, together with tomatoes, washed rice and seasonings. Simmer for one-half hour.

CARAMEL BLANC MANGE: 3 cups fresh or diluted evaporated milk, 6½ level tablespoons flour, 6 tablespoons sugar, ¼ teaspoon salt, ½ teaspoon vanilla.

Mix the flour, salt and ½ cup cold milk. Stir to a smooth paste. Meanwhile scald the rest of the milk. Pour a little of the scalded milk on the flour mixture and blend. Add this to the remaining milk and stir constantly over fire until the mixture coats the spoon.

Put the sugar in a frying pan over a low fire and stir until it is melted and a golden brown color. Remove from the fire, add slowly, stirring constantly, ¼ cup of boiling water. Return to the stove and stir until smooth. Add the caramelized sugar to the other mixture and cook for 10 or 15 minutes longer. Add the vanilla or other seasoning if desired and pour into cold, wet molds or glasses. When cold turn out on a sauce dish and serve with top milk.

Raw CARROT RELISH: Wash and scrape raw carrots and let stand in cold water until crisp. Drain well. Chop or grate the carrots, season with salt, pepper and a little dilute vinegar and serve. Instead of chopping or grating the carrots, they may be cut in long, thin strips and served like celery.

THURSDAY

Breakfast

Cornmeal Mush-Milk-Sugar, Whole Wheat Bread-Butter, Milk for Children, Coffee for Adults.

Dinner

Baked Beans-Baked Potatoes, Fresh Spinach, Bread-Butter, Baked Apple. For the young child put the beans through a sieve, combine with hot milk and serve as soup.

Supper

Creamed Spaghetti with Carrots, Whole Wheat Bread-Butter and Cheese, Stewed Apricots, Tea for Adults, Milk for Children.

CREAMED SPAGHETTI WITH CARROTS: 1½ cups broken spaghetti, 3 tablespoons margarine, 3 tablespoons flour,

½ teaspoon salt, ⅛ teaspoon pepper, 3 cups fresh or diluted evaporated milk, 1½ cups cooked carrots.

Clean and scrape carrots, cut in long, narrow slices and cook until tender in a small amount of boiling salted water. Cook the spaghetti until tender (about 25 mins.) in 3 quarts of boiling water to which has been added ½ teaspoon of salt. Drain.

Melt fat, add flour and seasonings and blend thoroughly. Pour on the milk and stir until thick and smooth. Cook for 5 minutes longer. Put ½ the spaghetti in a baking dish, cover with ½ the carrots, then add ½ the sauce. Repeat, using the remaining ingredients. Bake in a moderate oven for 15 to 20 minutes and serve.

FRIDAY

Breakfast

Oatmeal-Milk-Sugar, Whole Wheat Bread-Butter, Milk for Children, Coffee for Adults.

Dinner

Creamed Codfish, Spinach and Cabbage Salad, Boiled or Mashed Potatoes, Whole Wheat Bread-Butter, Fried

Mush-Syrup (Omit the fried mush for the small child), Milk for Children.

Supper

Baked Bean Soup, Whole Wheat Bread-Butter, Fresh Raw Apple, Tea for Adults, Milk for Children.

CREAMED CODFISH: 1 cup salt codfish, 1 cup milk, 1 egg, 2 tablespoons butter, 2 tablespoons flour.

Separate the fish into very small pieces and leave in cold water to cover for three hours, changing the water three times. Heat the milk in a double boiler. Add the codfish, well drained, and cook for ten minutes. Mix the butter with the flour until a smooth paste is formed, then stir it into the milk, stirring until thickened. Cook ten minutes. Take the dish from the heat, add the beaten egg, stir well and serve without further cooking, adding a sprinkling of pepper just before dishing. If the sauce is cooked after the egg is added, the milk is likely to curdle. The egg may be omitted.

FRIED MUSH: Pack cornmeal mush in a greased can or in a small bread pan; cool and cover; cut in slices and fry (sauté).

Baked Bean Soup: 3 cups cold baked beans, 3 cups water, 3 cups milk, salt and pepper, 2 level tablespoons flour, ¼ sliced carrot, 2 slices onion, 3 tablespoons fat.

Put beans, onion and carrot in saucepan with 3 cups water and allow to simmer for a half hour. Rub through a colander, or coarse sieve. Add milk, salt and pepper. Reheat and add flour and fat, which have been blended together. Let boil slowly for 10 minutes.

SATURDAY

Breakfast

Farina-Milk-Sugar, Bread-Molasses, Milk for Children, Coffee for Adults.

Dinner

Scalloped Potatoes in Tomato Sauce, Whole Wheat Bread-Butter, Cabbage Salad, Brown Sugar Pudding, Milk for Children.

Supper

Creamy Eggs on Toast, Whole Wheat Bread-Butter, Sliced Bananas-Top Milk, Milk for Children, Tea for Adults.

SCALLOPED POTATOES IN TOMATO SAUCE: 1¼ quarts sliced potatoes, 2 to 3 onions sliced, 2 cups strained tomato, 1½ teaspoons salt, ½ teaspoon pepper, 2 tablespoons flour.

Peel and slice potatoes, parboil one or two minutes in a small quantity of water, drain. Put a layer in a baking dish. Add onion, a sprinkle of salt, pepper and flour; repeat. The tomatoes may be diluted with the water in which potatoes were parboiled. Add tomatoes to potatoes, dot with fat, cover dish and bake 1½ hours or until done.

CREAMY EGGS ON TOAST: 2½ cups hot milk, 5 eggs, ¾ teaspoon salt, ⅛ teaspoon pepper, 1 teaspoon butter, 5 slices toast.

Beat eggs slightly, add salt and pepper. Stir hot milk into egg mixture and cook over hot water, stirring constantly until mixture is thick and creamy. Add butter. Serve on toast.

BROWN SUGAR PUDDING: 3 cups milk, 4½ tablespoons cornstarch, 4 tablespoons brown sugar, ¼ teaspoon salt, 1 egg, ½ teaspoon vanilla (1 teaspoon cornstarch may be substituted for the egg if desired).

Mix the cornstarch, salt, 2 tablespoons sugar and ½ cup cold milk. Meanwhile scald the rest of the milk in the top of a double boiler. Pour a little of the scalded milk on the cornstarch mixture and blend well. Add this to the remaining scalded milk and stir constantly until the pudding coats the spoon. Remove the spoon, cover the double boiler and cook for 25 minutes, stirring occasionally. Beat the egg slightly, add the remaining sugar and pour the pudding over the egg mixture gradually, stirring constantly (never add the egg to the hot mixture). Combine thoroughly and return to the double boiler to cook 1 minute longer. Add the vanilla, beat up well, and pour into cold, wet molds or sherbet glasses. Chill thoroughly. Serve with sliced stewed fruit or top milk, if desired.

SUNDAY

Breakfast

Tomato Juice for All, Oatmeal-Milk-Sugar, Whole Wheat Bread-Butter, Milk for Children, Coffee for Adults.

Dinner

Liver in Gravy, Baked Potatoes-Scalloped Onions, Whole Wheat Bread-Butter, Creamy Rice Pudding, Milk for Children.

Supper

Hashed Brown Potatoes, Buttered String Beans, Corn-
bread, Butter, Apricot Whip with Soft Custard, Cocoa
for All. The hashed brown potatoes, being fried, should
not be given to young children.

LIVER IN GRAVY: 1 pound beef or pork liver, 2 tablespoons flour, 1 teaspoon salt, ⅛ teaspoon pepper, 4
tablespoons drippings, 3 cups hot water, 1 slice onion,
minced.

Sprinkle slices of liver with salt and pepper, dredge
with flour, dip in milk and again in flour. Brown in
drippings, then add hot water and rest of seasonings.
Cover and simmer one hour. Remove meat, thicken
the liquid in the pan, season, and pour over the liver.

CORN CAKE: 1 cup cornmeal, ¾ cup flour, 3½ teaspoons baking powder, 1 teaspoon salt, ¼ cup molasses,
¾ cup milk, 1 egg or 2 egg yolks, 1 tablespoon melted
shortening.

Mix and sift dry ingredients. Combine milk and
molasses, beaten egg and shortening. Add this to dry
ingredients, stirring only until mixed. Bake in a shallow
buttered pan 20 minutes in a hot oven.

CREAMY RICE PUDDING: 4 cups fresh or diluted evaporated milk, ½ cup rice, ⅓ cup molasses, ½ teaspoon salt, ½ teaspoon cinnamon, 1 tablespoon butter.

Wash rice, mix ingredients, pour into buttered baking dish and bake 3 hours in a slow oven, stirring three times during the first hour to prevent settling. At the last stirring add the butter.

APRICOT WHIP: Stir two cups of stewed apricots which have a little juice, through a sieve. Fold into the cold apricot pulp the stiffly beaten whites of two eggs. Pile lightly in sauce dishes and serve.

Sleep is also very necessary to preserve health. Some people require more than others, but every one should have the amount which he or she requires. Some people as they grow older find it more and more difficult to sleep well. Of course, if they have cares and anxieties, it is hard to put them out of their minds and compose themselves to sleep, but if they can acquire the habit of reading not too exciting a book for a while; if they can remember to take enough exercise so that they will be physically tired; if they are a little careful about the covers under which they sleep—they should be warm and yet not too heavy—I think the average normal person observing these rules will be able to sleep an adequate number of hours, even though he may not achieve as much sleep as he would like to have. People who do not sleep should not worry about it. They should lie there and rest and think about pleasant things. They will either fall asleep or, at the worst, get up next morning perhaps a little less refreshed but still quite able to do their daily tasks and retire early the next night, usually to sleep.

Recreation is a very necessary part of health, for the mental side enters in here. No one who does not have a certain amount of recreation, let us say, can live a healthy mental life. One should have as many interests in the home as one possibly can. Besides a vocation, whatever it may be—even if it is that of housewife—try to have some avocation, something in life which occupies either your mind or your hands, which will change your trend of thought when you wish to change it. If a woman is on her feet a great deal performing household tasks, she should learn to do something which will keep her sitting and rest her, for in this restless age, even if it must be done by artificial means, it is necessary to acquire an atmosphere of peace for part of every day. It is necessary not only to one's own health but also to the happiness of those in the home.

Some of the men I know who lead a most active mental life get recreation at a carpenter's bench and some business men collect stamps all through their lives, or make collections of some other kind which require watching catalogues for sales and studying whatever particular thing they are interested in. And added to these interests which can be developed at home, every one should keep certain interests outside the home; something which will take them outside of themselves and which will make them take a wider view of life.

Work with some civic group, or some active piece of work for the community will make the world a far more interesting place to live in.

All these things have to do with normal life, and the keeping of oneself in good mental and physical condition, but to all of us no matter how careful we are, there come periods of illness. It seems to me that for the minor ailments every one is better off to be cared for at home, but in order to do this adequately, a mother must learn to be almost a trained nurse. I am often very much surprised at the absolute inexperience in caring for illness which is shown by the average young girl and it has always seemed to me a commentary on the mother's bringing up of that girl. Every girl before she starts her own home should know how to read a clinical thermometer, how to recognize the ordinary symptoms of illness, how to give an enema, how to look at a sore throat, how to make a bed with a person in it, how to give a person a bath in bed. With these things as a background, a woman can understand the doctor's orders and follow them out and it will not be necessary to go to a hospital for every minor ailment, or have a trained nurse or call in a doctor when he is not needed. With this amount of training in her youth, she can learn certain other things more easily as the need arises in her life, but in cases of serious illness or necessary operations, the hospital is undoubtedly the best place to be in.

As things are to-day the very rich and the very poor usually can have the best care in a hospital. The most difficult situation is that facing the person of average means. Our everyday man and woman who does not wish to accept charity, but who must live on a small income, finds illness of any kind a serious condition, but an illness which requires a doctor and hospital care is a calamity. In one or two places in this country this has been recognized. The need has been met by some public-spirited persons or by the community itself, but so far it is not generally planned for and hospital care cannot be obtained except at great expense if it is paid for at all. It is particularly hard for this group as they sometimes have to go either to a mediocre doctor and get poor care, or plunge unduly into debt to meet the necessary bills.

It seems to me that every young girl should not only have the general training for illness which I have already mentioned but should have some training to prepare her for child-bearing and for the caring of the baby when it arrives. Many and many a girl have I known who was completely without knowledge of what the most usual conditions surrounding this period of life were apt to be. A girl should know the normal way of living through the long nine months of pregnancy. She should know how to take care of herself, she should understand and make allowances for certain abnormalities of feelings and of nerves. The most normal human being ordinarily will not be completely normal through this rather trying experience and yet the more normal she makes her life, the better it will be for her.

Not only the girl but the young boy should be taught something which will fit him to be a husband and father. Many a young man enters upon his duties as a husband with no knowledge of the nature or of the feelings of a woman. He cannot be blamed if he does not understand, but those who fail to teach him are probably responsible for many unhappy marriages and both these young people should know something about the care of a baby if they are going to be given one to bring up, to educate and start on its way through life. There are books to-day that teach all this. They are worth reading but I would suggest that not only in the colleges of home economics but in every school and college there be given some practical instruction along these lines to both men and women.

I do not mean only knowing how to hold a baby, but a girl should also know how to bathe and dress and feed a baby, and there is no real reason why a boy should not be taught the underlying principles of the proper way of feeding a baby, of the importance of regularity, of sleep and of air and exercise. Early training will save him much difficulty later in life and he will be more patient with his wife and with his baby while this training is going on. A course in the psychology of child training would probably help the average boy and girl to train themselves.

Few people realize what a difference it makes in real illness if a child is taught certain rudimentary things, so that under a doctor's care he behaves himself properly and is a good patient. I have seen babies of one and two years refuse to look at the doctor, bury their heads in their mother's lap, wail before they had been touched, close their mouths when they were told to open them and in every way behave like the undisciplined infants they probably were.

On the other hand, a well-trained child will be cooperative and will obey whatever it is told to do, but it depends on the parents and not on the children, and the parents can only know what they should teach their children to do if they are taught themselves in their adolescent period. Even if young people do not marry, it is rare that they do not come in contact with children or with members of their families at some time when a certain knowledge of the ordinary rules of hygiene or medical care will be valuable, and as members of a household their usefulness will be greatly enhanced if knowledge along these health lines has been a part of their education.

To me it seems that one cannot lay too much emphasis on the necessity for planning family life in order that the health of the family may be kept on a high level. All the other conditions surrounding the family life depend fundamentally on the ability of that family to function normally physically.

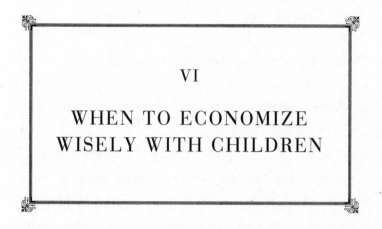

VI

WHEN TO ECONOMIZE WISELY WITH CHILDREN

BABYHOOD is the most important time in the life of any human being. It is generally conceded now that in a physical way the ground is laid before the age of six for the future health of the individual.

In the old days nobody thought it important to do anything about a baby's first teeth. To-day we know that the care of the first teeth is almost more important than taking care of the permanent teeth which come later.

All the habits which make for good health are begun in the first years of babyhood and to-day no mother has a right to fail to prepare herself before her baby is born by reading books and consulting her doctor in order that she may know at least theoretically what should be done for her baby, even though much, of course, can only come with experience and practice.

So much from the point of view of physical health.

There is another side, however, which is just as important and which must also be studied before a child is born, namely child psychology. There are so many things which have been discovered in the last thirty years on the subject of the influences in early babyhood which carry through into later life. We are only just beginning to realize how important is the mental and emotional life of a little child. You may plant the seeds for future nervousness and bad temper at three weeks of age. I heard a nurse not long ago, when complimented on the fact that the baby she was taking care of was a placid and smiling baby of nine months old, say quietly that all her babies were good babies, and on observation of her treatment I realized that it would naturally be so. She herself had a sweet and gentle and calm disposition. She rarely hurried, she was extremely punctilious about the baby's health, food and sleep and regularity, but she did not fuss about unnecessary things. She troubled her babies as little as possible and she allowed them as much pleasure as possible and they just developed naturally into calm and happy human beings.

Babies should not be disturbed when they are asleep, even to please grandmothers or aunts or friends. We should recognize early that a baby has as much right to his life, even though he may be for a time only a healthy little animal, as we have to ours. In the first year of a baby's life he learns more than in many, many years thereafter. Everything is a new experience and if we will only allow him to develop naturally instead of trying to hurry his development and bring him new experiences before he is ready for them, we will find that we have a more placid and a happier baby.

There is one thing which I would like to say to young parents: do not look for trouble. Trouble will come sometimes, a baby will be sick and you should be quick to notice any of the signs which mean real illness, but some of the children whom I know who are ill most of the time are those wrapped around in cotton wool. I always remember with joy a story of some poor little rich children who went into the street accompanied by two nurses and who were never allowed if they dropped a toy on the floor of their nursery to pick it up again, for fear they might acquire germs. Some one passing them on the street one day saw their nurses talking to the policeman and these carefully guarded darlings were licking a line along the stone building, acquiring probably more germs than they had ever encountered in their lives before!

Fear is a bad thing at all times and should be eliminated from our lives as much as possible.

The atmosphere created by the people around little children will react very quickly on them and so remember if you are bringing up a baby that it is important for you to watch your own discipline. You must not lose your temper if your baby is to be good-tempered and placid. There is much truth in some of the time-worn jokes. In very truth a child does bring up not only his father but his mother too.

I would like to emphasize again the value to the mother and father as well as to the child, of mothers caring for their own children at least at some period of their lives, preferably during the first year. Of course, this is advice which the average woman does not need because she knows that when her baby is born, she is going to have to take care of it herself. Even when the circumstances of the parents allow them to have a nurse, they lose much of the joy if they do not themselves do everything for the baby. Besides, the average young mother and father are timid and willing to rely on the judgment of somebody more experienced. It is in order to get over this idea and develop their own self-reliance as far as the children are concerned that I would urge them to accept this responsibility without any outside assistance.

However, if the mother has to work as well as the father and economic necessity makes it advisable for her to provide some one to look after her child, that person should be chosen with extreme care. If it is a neighbor, be sure that she has the qualities of mind and heart and intelligence which will make it possible for her to bring up your baby in the way you would do it yourself. And remember how vitally important are those first years and that the qualities of the person coming in close contact with your child make an indelible impression on that child's mind.

Every child should have periodic examinations by a doctor in order to make sure that he is kept in good health. The same general rules apply to children as to adults but they must have more air, more sleep, better food more carefully chosen and carefully cooked, and a greater amount of exercise.

I have seen children thrive under adverse conditions when these rules were closely adhered to. For instance, I have known small children, who because of the circumstances of their parents had to spend the first years of their lives summer and winter in New York City in small apartments or tenements, to thrive because their lives were intelligently ordered. They were given proper food, slept long hours, went out to the park on hot summer days and stayed there in the shade of the trees from early morning till fairly late evening, only spending the hottest part of the day in the house, and they lived regular lives. Some children whom I knew were born in South America under very difficult climatic conditions and yet because of common-sense and intelligence in their upbringing, they are healthy, strong young people to-day.

The average family is obliged to economize as much as they can, on their children as well as on everything else. I would, however, urge very strongly that there be no economy in milk, but that the necessary cuts be made in the children's clothes. The amount spent by the average family on dress can easily be curtailed and with a little ingenuity, a homemade dress will bring a child as much pleasure as anything bought in the most expensive shop.

If possible give a child books, then teach him how to use the library, and whether he has books of his own or not take him to see the books which are written and illustrated for children and which will remain in his mind as an educational asset. Teaching the use of a library at an early age is perhaps one of the most valuable things that we can do for a small child to-day.

It is often said by foreigners that American children are spoiled. Perhaps this is so and it is certain that many parents felt as long as we were prosperous whatever the children wanted, they must have, regardless of what the parents' financial situation might be. Perhaps the depression has brought about a certain amount of very salutary discipline. Bribing children to do what they should do is one of the signs of poor discipline and allowing children to be a burden to everybody around them because they have not learned consideration for others and have no ability to entertain themselves, is a sign that the parents of those children have miserably failed in their ability to put interests into the lives of their children. The children of to-day do not have as much candy as in the past, therefore it is not used as a bribe in the way it frequently used to be, but other bribes are often used.

It is far better to inculcate early into every child certain definite habits of discipline. Then they will not try to get what they want by crying for it or by making themselves disagreeable, because they know it is a useless performance on their part and while they sometimes may forget the habits started at an early age, it is astonishing how quickly these habits return when the need arises and the opportunity for settling back into their usual surroundings comes again.

If a child is trained in the habits of cleanliness, methodical care of clothes and room, and given certain tasks in the house to perform which accustom them young to the idea that they have work in the world, they will find association with other young people easier and take up their responsibilities in life infinitely more easily than if they leap straight from a home where everything has been done by mother and father for them, into an environment where they must depend on themselves.

Once children begin to go to school, the attitude of the parents must be, if possible, that they are engaged in their first responsible piece of work. School is for them what work is for their fathers and mothers. For the time being it is their task in the world. If possible, there should be close cooperation between the home and the school so that parents will know what the teachers are trying to do for their children and cooperate with them in order that the children may get the best out of their school years.

For this reason I have always felt that the parent-teacher associations are a very valuable asset to the life of the children during their school years. If it is possible for the parents and teachers to get together and agree on certain things for the children at this time, such for instance, as regular hours for going to bed, school luncheons, no movies except over the week-ends and the type of books that the children shall read, I think we will find the early school years of greatly increased value to all children.

In considering a child's schooling, be sure to consider any natural aptitudes which the child may have. The child may love music or art, and while the talent will not be sufficient to make it a professional occupation for the future, he should be encouraged in school to develop this talent so that he may have more appreciation of beauty and achievement in these arts, and perhaps develop an avocation which may bring a great deal of pleasure if no actual financial remuneration. Some children have a gift for languages, and if you discover that, they should be allowed to develop it as much as possible for it may be of great value to them later on in life. All parents should remember that modern languages are best learned by little children, for then they learn them entirely by ear just as they learn to talk and they know by instinct what is right and what is wrong, and they do not have to reason or remember innumerable rules of grammar. The accent in foreign languages is apt to be better if the language is acquired in early youth. Some people go on acquiring new languages all through their lives but these are exceptional cases. I have always been thankful that French was almost a second native tongue to me. I actually spoke it before I spoke English. There have been many occasions when it has made understanding and friendship with other people possible which would have been impossible without this knowledge. Manual training for most children is of vital necessity and there are many kinds of manual work in which the child can express creative instinct which is one of the vital necessities in school.

An appreciation of nature is something which we should ordinarily think every child would acquire by himself. This is not true. We can give all children very great enjoyment and knowledge which will make the country a much more interesting place for them, if we will take the trouble to see that they learn about birds and animals and flowers and trees in early youth. Along with this appreciation and love of nature will go a valuable lesson in conservation. They will learn that if sportsmen constantly take life and do not preserve the young families of birds and beasts, whole species become extinct and sport vanishes. If one cuts down all the trees around because one enjoys the exercise, one will be without shade, and if such operations are extensive enough the water supply will be dried up unless wherever a tree is cut another is planted.

Germany and France and England have learned their lesson in conservation and where one sees a hillside denuded of large trees one invariably finds it replanted with new ones, and though Englishmen love their sport they take great care to observe the laws laid down for the preservation of animal and bird life.

All these lessons can be tied up with the child's understanding of patriotism and love of country. One does not destroy what nature gives us to love and conserve. When a man loves his country he does not launch into a war which is going to destroy thousands of young men if there is any way in which that war can be prevented.

Good citizenship can be taught in so many ways to these children in school. It is the duty of parents and teachers to see that into a child's consciousness gradually grow these interests of the greater world and an understanding of good citizenship and what responsibilities toward the community and the country mean.

I would also like to put in a plea that parents, when children come home with weird and wild tales of what terrible things have been done to them in school, will at least give the teachers the benefit of the doubt and go and talk the situation over with them before they tell the children that they feel sure they have been unjustly treated. There are often times when parents need to interpret their children to teachers, but there are times occasionally when teachers can find faults or good qualities which may not show up at home. Therefore, I would beg all parents, before they make any rash statements to the children, to go and talk things over with the teachers.

The health of children should, of course, be carefully guarded both in school and at home. These are the years when bad habits may be formed and when it is most important that good food, a sufficient amount of fresh air, exercise and sleep should be building up strong constitutions to meet the life work of the years to come.

In many communities there is a great lack of knowledge particularly among the young mothers as to child hygiene and the care and feeding of children. It seems to me that if it is possible for the home and the school to cooperate so that young mothers may be educated as to their children's physical needs, and follow that education up with an understanding of their mental and emotional needs, it will mean a great deal to the success of school life and the solving of many of the problems of youth which cause a great many people worry to-day.

A very wise man once told me that he was glad he had been trained in his youth to be a biologist and he thinks that a great many of our young families would do better to learn a certain amount of biology in order that they may be more helpful to their children.

Try to understand young people, particularly your adolescent young people, and not to be shocked or irritated by them. They are at an age where they do not understand themselves or the emotions which sweep over them and it is a time above all times when wise parents may be useful.

We should try above everything else to keep away from all children any sense of fear, in these early years. Fear of their teachers, fear of the ridicule of their contemporaries, fear of their own inability to meet whatever situations they may have to face in life. I have always found that children were happier if they were allowed to have something which made them distinctly like all other children, than if they were obliged to express the individuality of their elders. Children, on the whole, are too young to be individual. They like to fit into the landscape and it is better to let them do so.

When the time comes for the child to go to work, if his preparation has been carefully planned, he will be better fitted to enter into a competitive world that surrounds him in the professions, industries, agriculture or whatever it may be that he takes up. At the moment we are seeking to keep our young people in school a little bit longer because places for them are so scarce and it is most discouraging for them to move out into a world which obviously does not wish to receive them and where they are in competition immediately with people who have more experience than they have. Under certain conditions it is necessary for children to go to work because the burden of their care no longer can be borne by the older members of the family and when it looks as though this might be the case it is important to have it in mind during these early years when they are being prepared for the work of the future. The habits which have been formed, will eventually make the dispositions and characters, which will ultimately mean men and women unhappy, inadequate, afraid, or men and women happy in their work and able to meet life serenely and courageously.

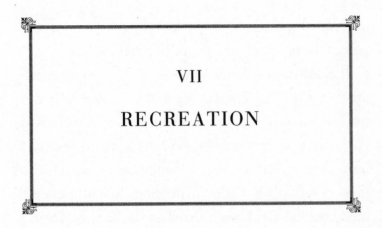

VII

RECREATION

In our chapter on budgets we touched on the amount allowed for recreation in the family budget but it seems to
me that it is well to enlarge a little on this subject, for after
all a good part of the life of the family is concerned with
recreation.

The day's work must be carried on by all the adults, in
factory, office or home. The children, from the time they
begin to go to school, have their work in the school and,
on their return home, the preparation of their lessons and
their share of household tasks. Even a very small child
should have certain tasks which can be considered work

and yet recreation should be looked upon as an essential part of the hours which are not the working hours.

It is just as important to young and old to have recreation as it is to have work. We in this country have never really considered recreation as an integral part of everyday life as have other countries and I think that is because we have been so busy making a living that we have had less time to really live. Older civilizations live in a more leisurely fashion and know more about recreation. There are few English people who do not have an avocation as well as a vocation and a hobby of some kind. Sometimes our hobbies are almost as hard work as our real work, but they serve the purpose of changing the current of thought, and therefore they are just as restful as though a person sat down and folded his hands.

Some of the busiest people we know are rested primarily by the fact that their occupations are varied and their minds are constantly changing from one subject to another so that they do not have time to be wearied by any one monotonous occupation.

The world over, certain people—working people so called—have had little time for recreation but with the changes now looming up (we are talking at present of a forty-hour week for people in factories) it will mean much more time for leisure and much more interest in the types of recreation which we will enjoy. Many people will find themselves without any resources for this unwonted amount of leisure and that is one of the things that we ought to consider in the bringing up of our children. They should not be allowed to grow up without developing a number of interests which can in turn develop into recreations when they grow older and have to settle down to one occupation as their work.

I have known many people who worked in offices all day whose recreation was working in a garden before they left in the morning and when they got home in the evening and who spent many winter evenings poring over catalogues, planning the next summer's garden of flowers and vegetables.

I have known other people who could wander along for hours in the country with a pair of field-glasses and return with a book full of notes on the birds which they had seen. One of the best known figures in England to-day when she wants recreation chooses a congenial friend, straps a frying pan and kettle around her waist, puts a few clothes in a rubber sheet across her shoulders and goes off to camp on some nearby hill or on the banks of some small stream. On these trips some favorite book is always handy or a sketching pad.

Anything you learn to do which is not your regular work may turn out to be a recreation, but one thing is certain that in this new world which we are making to-day, recreation is going to be more important than it has ever been before and people must be able to develop hobbies and avocations of every kind.

If you begin to collect, you will find it a very absorbing avocation and your fellow collectors will range from people who collect different kinds of buttons to Mr. Morgan, who collects the most valuable books and pictures in the world.

A child must have part of its recreation every day out-of-doors. Exercise should be made recreation if possible and if the child lives in the country on a farm some of the chores which fall to his or her lot may become recreation if that child is properly trained in love of the outdoors and in the knowledge of nature and love of animals. To teach a child when young to observe and to have eyes to see in the country will add enormously to his enjoyment and his recreation. It is not only Maeterlinck who can derive lessons from watching the bees. It is easier in the country or in a small town or village to keep the recreation for both young and old on a simple basis and the greater simplicity is an advantage. The fact that one has to exercise more originality and ingenuity in providing recreation is, I think, one of the great advantages of living in a small place or in a rural community. Children can be trained to enjoy many things if their elders enjoy them too. Books can be real recreation and will undoubtedly be enjoyed by the young if they are valued by the older members of the family. The radio can provide good music, interesting talks and many things of great value to home life. Constant use of the radio may be annoying, but this depends entirely upon the individual family and its tastes and selections, and here again the influence of the older members of the group will be the deciding factor.

If you live in the city you have to take, of course, a great deal more trouble to get an appreciation of outdoor life and the enjoyment of it, but just because more of an effort is needed, sometimes it is more greatly appreciated.

I think that one of the first things which a family ought to do is to find certain recreations and pleasures which they can enjoy as a family and where young and old do not have to be separated. Games which can be played by all the family are always to be encouraged whether they are games at home or games out-of-doors. I have seen baseball teams made up of boys and girls and men and women and sometimes I have seen a woman or a girl who could bat as well as any member of the male sex. This certainly can provide many a healthy and happy Saturday afternoon for a family whether they live in the city and go out to some country field to play—or whether they actually live in the country. Hide and seek, prisoner's base and many others are outdoor diversions as long as you can run. There are many other outdoor games which can be played quietly.

There is no reason why young and old should not go to the movies and theaters together and why they should not go to dances together. I know that the tendency is for the young at present to prefer to be alone. This is partly to get away from supervision and to feel independent, and partly due to the fact that so many older people when they are at parties with the young, assume a critical attitude which destroys all freedom of relationship between the generations.

In European countries you will often see in the summer holidays whole families starting on a walking trip together. They carry small bags on their backs which contain a change of shoes and stockings, a sweater, a tooth brush and night clothes and nothing else. Yet, with this they walk several days through the Swiss or Tyrolese Alps, or along some picturesque river. There is no hurry about it but quite a bit of ground is covered in a day and on the way they sing, and sing very delightfully. They stop for lunch at some little wayside inn; they stop for coffee in the afternoon in some little garden under the trees and in the evening they stop again for dinner and the night. You see them all out-of-doors, the men smoking their pipes and the women with their knitting, having as good a time as if they were spending hundreds of dollars and covering the ground in the most expensive motor cars.

I have seen the same type of walking trips in the Scotch Highlands and in the English Lake District, and you may come across parties on bicycle trips or on canoe trips. Stevenson, you will remember, canoed through Holland.

We are getting more used over here to going camping in our holidays and I think it is one of the very best signs, and augurs well for the health and simplicity of future generations.

There is another thing that holidays spent in this way accomplish—they cement by little homely memories and jokes and foolish happenings the association of a family or of a group of friends. They make for intimacy which may be dangerous if the people are not really congenial, and I would advise you to stay away from camping trips and walking trips if you are doubtful about your friends! If you do get on well together, however, you will find an additional joy forever afterwards in the memory of an early swim in the lake with the sun just coming over the hill, or of a beautiful sunset which colored the sky as you paddled your boat into camp after a long day of fishing or of exploring the neighboring waterways.

It is good for those of us who live in the east, even though we do know our own hills and streams, to go when we can and take a trip in our western parks. This is being made less and less expensive owing to the fact that the railroads provide one with round-trip tickets at greatly reduced rates during the summer months and if we learn to look after ourselves and to be contented with simple accommodations it need not be an extravagant trip. By motor it can be done for even less money and if time is a consideration the airplane can be called in to accelerate the trip.

There is real joy in knowing our beautiful country and in knowing how, through exercising a little ingenuity, we can get a great deal for a comparatively moderate sum of money. Knowing our own country is something which, while we can consider it recreation, is closely allied to a duty, for it is necessary for good citizenship that we should attempt to visualize the vastness of our country and the multiplicity of interests amongst our people. In periods of prosperity it is possible for young people to earn their way on a trip of this kind by working a few days here and there for hospitable farmers.

The number of things which provide recreation without cost have increased greatly with the knowledge and appreciation which our education gives us. Some people care nothing about music, but if you do care about it, there is no country in the world where you can have better music free or at a low cost than you can in this country.

We have some of the most beautiful collections of pictures that can be found anywhere in the world in our various cities, for the enjoyment of those who have an appreciation and a love for pictures. I am often struck with the fact that very few people who live in New York City, for instance, know of the opportunities which the city provides and which are really varied enough for every taste. Many evenings can be spent with interest and profit and pleasure if we have sufficient appreciation to get pleasure through our eyes and ears.

I always feel that education should open as many avenues as possible to us so that we may have as many ways of obtaining recreation and enjoyment as possible.

As we grow older our recreation must of necessity change in character but there is a tendency in many of us to give up things which we like to do at a much younger age than is really necessary. I had an old friend of eighty-three years who still rode leisurely through her tobacco fields in Kentucky and when asked if she was not too old to ride, she answered that having never stopped riding it had never occurred to her to give it up.

After all, much enjoyment is simply keeping the spirit which makes it possible for us to enjoy things. That spirit requires cultivation and with our added leisure I hope that we will all come to cultivate it and that our people will prove a more agreeable and truly educated people because of their ability to enjoy recreation.

VIII

MODERN FAMILY
CONDITIONS

THE economic conditions of the last few years have, I think, had one good effect at least. They have drawn children and parents even in well-to-do families more closely together because in times of illness it has not been possible to have trained nurses, and for purposes of recreation and at certain times in each day the mother has found herself obliged to relieve the nurse and this has brought better understanding of her children and closer supervision. We must all realize, I think, that between generations there is a tremendous gulf and that each new generation sets up its own standards as the result of contact with its own contemporaries. No mother can force her ideals and opinions upon her children though her experiences and her influence may enter into their consciousness and help to form their point of view. The deciding factor in each generation's actions will always be, however, the thought of their own generation and their actions will be largely ruled by the world conditions in which they live.

What would have seemed to one generation absolutely immoral will to another generation simply seem a matter of custom and manners and therefore in a changing world we must bear in mind that we cannot be too sure that ideals which have served us in the past are to continue to serve us in the future.

The woman's relationship with her children and her husband may be undergoing a change because women are carrying on outside work and assuming positions with the men in the world of professional and public life in a way which is of necessity changing the home relationship.

Just what it is all going to mean in the future none of us knows as yet, but that the family will persist in some form or other seems inevitable because human needs and cravings seem to be answered best by this association. Even in

Russia where such determined effort was made to change their form of social life, to wipe out the family and establish professional homes where children should be brought up all together, it has proved a failure and the unit of the family still persists.

We do see to-day, however, a completely changing attitude toward divorce on the part of the younger generation. It is no longer expected that either men or women will sacrifice their lives to an unhappy mistake.

I personally think that probably it would be wiser if marriage were made far more difficult. We are constantly agitating the question of whether there should be uniform divorce laws, but I think it would be more to the point to discuss the question of under what conditions and restrictions people should marry. Any one thinking seriously about this question from the point of view not only of the mature individuals involved but of children will acknowledge the fact that nothing can be worse for children than to grow up in a home where the atmosphere is one of unhappy and constant bickering.

There is no question but that it is better for children to have a father and a mother who will bring them up in a sympathetic and unifying way, but if what one parent wishes the other parent takes pleasure in destroying, there is no question but that the result will be chaos in the mind of the child. If a man and woman marry and have children and find themselves uncongenial, but are able to keep their home life gracious and bring their children up without a consciousness of disagreement or of bitterness, then it is undoubtedly better for divorce not to be considered, but this requires exceptional people and conditions and cannot easily be done. It seems to me that the worst possible results are obtained when a child is torn between two separate homes. If there must be a divorce or separation, then one or the other parent should be given jurisdiction, but the parent not having the child actually living with it, should, of course, have the right to see the child and occasionally have its companionship.

That two people who do not find each other congenial should be obliged to live together is not common-sense according to the thought of some of the modern generation. There are still many people besides those of the Catholic faith who do not agree with this, more particularly perhaps among the older generation, but it is well for us all at least to acknowledge that such ideas are more or less in the air and to give them consideration. They may never become particularly prevalent but some changes are bound to come and therefore people of all ages should be thinking and discussing what on the whole is going to be best for the social life and the family life of the future. The ostrich is never preserved from destruction by burying its head in the sand!

It seems a far cry from whether a married woman shall work, to our attitude toward divorce and the family in general, but as a matter of fact these things are all closely interwoven. I do not think that because women work, divorce will become more prevalent but because of the differences in the conditions under which we live to-day I think divorces are more apt to come just as I think women are more apt to hold jobs.

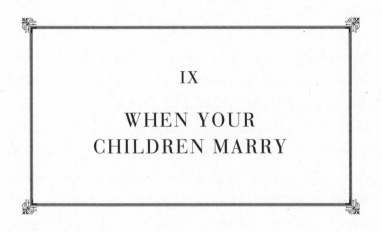

IX

WHEN YOUR CHILDREN MARRY

INEXTRICABLY tied up with the question of home conditions is the question of the right of women to have individual lives of their own and also the question of what the woman shall do whether she holds a job or not, when her children grow up and marry. If she has held a job, she will have something to turn to which will fill her life and make the transition far easier for her, for undoubtedly the relationship must change when the children marry.

If a woman has been a very possessive mother, it will be extremely difficult to turn over the possession of either her son or her daughter to some other person. The possessive type of mother love is the one great danger which threatens the relationship between mothers and the young married people. Perhaps in the old days there was still so much to do in the home that women had little or no time to interfere in the new household as it started out, or perhaps these new households pushed further into new country and transportation being so difficult, months and years went by without any visits between the old and the new homes. Holding a job may be a substitute for being unable to be with our children too much after they have started out for themselves. In any case this period in a woman's life is perhaps the greatest test of her character.

Up to this time, in all probability, she has felt herself entitled to claim much of her children's time and attention and she has taken the lead in their lives. If they were ill, they naturally came to her, and there is nothing in the world as gratifying as feeling that those whom you love not only love you, but need you and expect you to share whatever touches their lives.

A wise mother, however, will begin very early to face the fact that she cannot possess and control every moment of her children's lives. She will, as they grow up, encourage the brothers and sisters to depend upon each other, realizing that often two people of the same generation can be more helpful and understanding of each other than can any one of the older generation. She will encourage her children to have friends, real friends, not acquaintances, and while she will always try to share their joys and sorrows, she will not want to do so to the exclusion of every one else, and just as soon as the physical care of her children and her home makes it possible she will begin to build up interests of her own so that she will not be entirely dependent upon her children to fill her hours of leisure.

I believe very strongly that it is better to allow children too much freedom than too little; it is better for them to get their feet wet than to be told at the age of fifteen to put on their rubbers. They should be old enough by that time to take care of themselves and if they prefer to get their feet wet, they should be allowed to do so.

I think a great many mothers who nag their children about little things would find their relationship improved and their advice sought in more important things if they could remember that the five-year-olds they dressed and undressed and fed have grown to independent manhood and womanhood.

The line, of course, between interest and prying curiosity is sometimes hard to draw, but once the children are grown, while I would be always willing to listen if they wanted to talk, I think it is best to do very little questioning. You are apt to know a great deal more about your children if you let them volunteer their own information than if they think you are trying to check on all they do.

When it comes to their marrying, there is little that you can do. You can welcome the girl or boy that your boy or girl is interested in, let them come into the family and see how they show up in the family circle. Give them, under your supervision, all possible opportunities to see and know each other before they take the important step, but when they are once married, leave them alone. The first year of married life is bound to be a year of adjustment. No matter how well two people have known each other beforehand, meeting every day across the table over the breakfast coffee is a degree of intimacy which brings out many unknown traits. Again you must retain a receptive attitude, but try to make your son-in-law and your daughter-in-law feel that you are not trying to shape their lives. Young people need help, but they do not need criticism or interference.

Sometimes young people marry too young to know fully whether they are suited to each other, or how they will develop in the future, but this is something which they do not realize at the time. No amount of argument on the part of the elders ever seems to convince the younger generation and so we have to remember that only experience can teach certain things in life.

The older generation, when we were young, thought it their duty to advise us, but I doubt if we were any more really affected by it though we listened more attentively than would our children to-day.

Each generation must learn by its own experience and though it may be hard to watch our children go through the same mistakes which we went through, it will do no good to pursue them with warnings drawn from our own experience. All we can do is to be worthy of their confidence and to refrain from criticism and recriminations and then in the words of the Scripture we may be "a very present help in time of trouble."

More than this we cannot hope to be. We cannot expect to shape their ideas or in fact to shape the world which they are going to live in. All we can hope to do is to make them feel that they must be honest with themselves and honest with those they care about, living up to what they think is right and remembering always that we are not the judges of what is going to make the world a better place for them to live in. That we must leave to the judgment of the generation that comes after us.

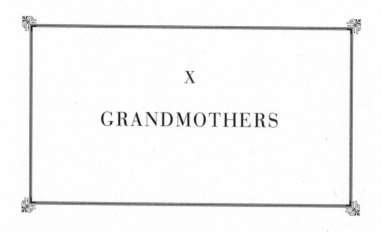

X

GRANDMOTHERS

ONE of my correspondents the other day asked me what I really thought the position of grandmothers was to-day. In her letter she said that she had read all there was to say on the subject of not interfering with your children when they were grown, and on letting them shoulder their own responsibilities, and on having plenty of interests which you could turn to so as not to be a burden on children, and so that even if they had to help you financially, at least they should not feel that they had to provide you with constant companionship and entertainment. She still felt, however, that it might be nice for grandchildren to know occasionally where they could find their grandmother.

This awakened a chord of sympathy in my own breast, for I sometimes think that as we grow older we should try to be restful. One of the most delightful persons I ever knew was a woman who probably meant more to many people than most of us do in this world and who was tied to her chair in a small New England village. She suffered a great deal and she had certain physical handicaps which would make most of us hermits, unable to think of anything but our own afflictions and disabilities and quite uninterested in the world at large. She was different; she knew everything that was happening; she had as keen a mind and as good judgment as any one I have ever known. Young and old flocked to her for her advice and stimulation; people would travel hours for an hour of her company.

One left her presence with the feeling of having been with a really great personality and in the presence of the kind of courage which makes one aspire to be courageous no matter what one's own difficulties or trials may be.

I think too many of us forget that as we grow older it is not so important what we do, because our place in the world is somewhat different from what it was when we were young. Then we were still carrying the burden of the work of the world. As we grow older it is much more important that we be something which furnishes youth with stimulation and courage and, occasionally, when youth is a little too hotheaded, with a word of restraint, though I do not favor much restraint.

I would always be with the mother who said she discovered that she was always saying "no" to her children, so one day she turned around and instead of saying "Johnnie, do not eat with your fingers," she said, "Johnnie, do eat with your spoon." I would far rather, instead of saying, "Reuben, do not jump off the cliff," say, "Reuben, why not try to get down it with a rope?"

So I think it is well for grandmothers to create an atmosphere of repose at least for part of the time. If they are well and strong and have the opportunity and the desire to run around the world now and then, perhaps it is well to do so, for their grandchildren may miss the haven of rest. If an older person is sympathetic and understanding, I think it is sometimes easier to bridge two generations than one. The zest of living is still too near the mother, and the children may feel more at ease with the repose of the grandmother. Of course, in some of the older civilizations like China and France, a grandmother rules the family. That is perhaps a mistake also, for too much authority makes the best of us autocratic. Being a good grandmother may require a certain amount of restraint and a good deal of unselfishness, for you must not spoil youth with too much kindness and you must never take the place of father and mother and give the children the feeling that they can turn to you as against their parents. These questions of family relationships are a little like tight-rope walking. The way is narrow and to balance yourself you must indeed be an acrobat. Tact and unselfishness will see you through, and it is perhaps a wise provision of nature which makes you as you grow older gradually feel detached yourself from the world's emotions.

Our joys are not so great but neither are our sorrows or our disappointments. We can be much more calm as we meet the accidents of life and therefore of more use to our grandchildren. We cannot sit in a corner of the fireplace with a cap on our head and knit from morning to night any more, but we can have a fireplace and a tea table and sit there now and then and our own grandchildren and our young friends will come to recognize an atmosphere where their coming means a pleasure and where their problems, joyous or sorrowful, will be the only subject of interest if they so desire.

It is a remarkable thing that few people when they are young or even middle-aged are really good listeners, or care primarily to hear what other people have to say. They are constantly breaking in with some contribution of their own and the younger they are the more anxious they are to hold the center of the stage. The reason that my old New England lady with all her physical handicaps was so satisfying to all the young people who flocked around her, was that she never talked about her own ailments; she knew that they were so bad that talking about them would make them no better. Her problems were fairly well worked out and she was interested enough to give these young things her full attention, and I have often left her realizing that most of the time she had adroitly urged me on to talk. She had made me clear in my own mind and only when I asked for her opinion or advice had it been given and then with great gentleness and moderation, never very critically, and with a suggestion only of restraint. For instance, I remember once asking her whether she believed that Mrs. Grundy's opinions and conventionalities would always be observed and she answered that the conventionalities of life had been built up for the safeguarding of the ordinary run of human beings; that some people could never be bound by rules of any kind or judged by them but that you were safe if you never were ashamed of anything you did.

The modern grandmother cannot be the old-fashioned grandmother, but she can contribute much to the world of to-day, and I personally have been extremely grateful in the past for the friendship and wisdom of some grand-mothers I have known. I hope that in the future there may be some young people who will find in my generation grandmothers to serve them in the same way.

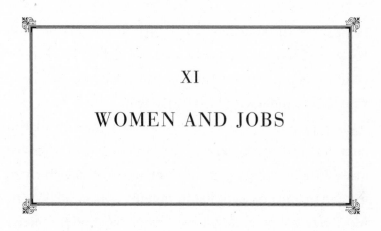

XI

WOMEN AND JOBS

Nowadays there is a great deal of agitation as to whether married women should work or not and in order to consider the question, I think we should go back a little bit further and consider whether women should work at all.

There was a time when very few women worked outside of their homes. All women were brought up with the feeling that a woman's place was in the home. She must marry, and if she did not marry, she had no work in the world, and we have in many old novels a picture of the maiden lady left to live at home, being more or less of a drudge, whiling away her time looking after the younger members of the family with very little attention from any-body, and having all her work accepted as a matter of course in return for the kindness of the man of the family who provided her with food and lodging.

This is not a pretty picture nor one that we like to contemplate but we must have it in our minds when we discuss the modern status of women, even though there were many instances of happy maiden aunts and cousins who were happy and beloved. From this condition the women have gradually risen in consideration largely as they gained economic independence for themselves and could provide financial help in the homes. For some time, of course, it has been necessary for the girl in many families to go to work at a fairly early age. Nowadays an effort is being made to keep young people a little longer out of the working field. This affects women as it does men, but more and more women are going to work every year and because of that we must look upon it not as an academic question, but as an actual situation which is with us to stay in the industrial world and in the average family.

Even where the young girl could be supported at home, she wants to register her own personality and to develop her own interests, and she spends for her clothes or for some interest of her own a part of the money which she is able to earn. Usually every girl pays part of her earnings for food and lodging even when she lives at home, and many a girl puts in all that she earns to support not only herself but some other members of her family. If it is not a father or a mother, it may be the education of some younger brother or sister that she is carrying.

In my own experience I am constantly surprised to find that many single women who are supposed to have only themselves to take care of are really supporting one or more other persons. Very often the boy in the family marries young and one girl stays at home either because she prefers her life with her parents or with whichever parent is still living, or because her feeling of duty to the older generation is often stronger than that of the boy in the family and keeps her from marrying until she feels she is not needed at home.

As a rule when a woman keeps on working after her marriage, it is a matter of necessity—not always an economic necessity, but sometimes the necessity of feeling that she is still able to do something which expresses her own personality even though she may be a wife and mother.

I never like to think of this subject of a woman's career and a woman's home as being a controversy. It seems to me perfectly obvious that if a woman falls in love and marries, of course her first interest and her first duty is to her home, but her duty to her home does not of necessity preclude her having another occupation. A woman, just like a man, may have a great gift for some particular thing. That does not mean that she must give up the joy of marrying and having a home and children. It simply means, when we set them in opposition to each other, that we haven't as yet grown accustomed to the fact that women's lives must be adjusted and arranged for in just the same way that men's lives are. Women may have to sacrifice certain things at times—so do men.

When the keeping of a home took all the strength and time that a woman had, the home was the factory where much that we now buy ready-made had to be manufactured. Few of us realize that only a little over a hundred years ago all the candles and soap and food used by the household in winter as well as in summer were prepared by the women of the house; all the linen and all the wool were made in the home; practically all the clothes both for men and women were made at home; all the washing was done at home.

I have a piece of linen made in Dutchess County from flax that was grown in the county and nowadays the art is completely lost. The necessity has gone to-day and therefore there are few women who have been in this country more than a short time and whose husbands earn more than the bare necessities of life, who are not able to do something besides keeping their home. They may choose to play bridge, or golf, or they may choose to do some part-time work or even full-time work in some job that interests them. If so—the only people to be concerned about it are the members of the family. To be sure, sometimes children resent the fact that their mother has a job and is not at their beck and call at any hour of the day or night. This is only so, of course, when her work is not needed for the necessities of life. But granted that the father provides the necessities, sometimes the children are jealous of the fact that a mother should want any interests outside of theirs. They are justified if something really vital goes out of their lives, but if their physical needs are cared for and if their mother, on her return, has enough vitality to keep in touch with their daily lives and know what has happened to them and to give them her sympathetic interest and advice, then it is probably better for the future lives of these children that they should have to exercise a little unselfishness, a little thought for themselves and for others because their mother is not always on hand. They have a right to expect that if they have a problem she will listen to it, but they have no right to expect that she will give up that which she loves and which is constructive and creative work, because they would like to have her home at five o'clock instead of at six o'clock. It might be fair to ask her to give up pure recreation but not a thing which really makes her an individual.

Do not make the mistake of thinking when you are married you need make no further effort about your family relations. The very best thing that comes to a woman with a job is the fact that she has to use her brains in order to find time for both her job and her home duties. This keeps her brain from stagnating. She has something new to talk to her husband about and he never will get the feeling that she is just like the old chair which he has always sat in—comfortable, but thoroughly familiar and never very interesting in consequence. The job of being a homekeeper, a wife and a mother plus some other job or some other work is quite a job. If any woman has the health and vitality and the desire to do both, it seems to me that it ought to make for a happier relationship at home instead of a discontented one.

In the emergency we are passing through, however, I am getting innumerable appeals asking that married women be not allowed to hold jobs which might be filled by married men or single men and women. That point of view is perhaps necessary during an emergency and it may be necessary for a woman to relinquish voluntarily her work if the man is earning enough for the family to live on, but as a permanent concession to the needs of society I rebel, for it seems to me that we have built up our nation on the theory that work is honorable; that those who can do something creative and productive may be doing some intangible good to their own souls, which, if they were not allowed to express themselves in work, might mean a loss to themselves in enrichment of personality, and in their happiness, and therefore, in the end, a loss to the community at large.

The problem is always an individual one which every woman must decide for herself, but if a woman wants to work and keep her home, let me beg you, Mr. Man, to help her and not hold her back. If you are sympathetic and understanding, you will find her in the end a better help-mate and your cooperation will mean a better and happier understanding between you. If you fight her she may be resentful, though she may give in to you, and you may wake up some day to find that you have a wife in your home who is an automaton—no longer a fulfilled and happy personality.

After all, as I have said, most women work from neces-sity because more money is needed in the home or because they feel the urge to do something definitely for the good of themselves if not for the public at large. It may possibly be that there are certain things that may lack constant supervision because the woman of the household has defi-nite hours of work outside her home, but I doubt whether the children of to-day will actually see any less of their mothers who work than do the children of the more or less leisure group of people who devote a great deal of time to amusement.

Of course, the mother who takes entire charge of her own children will not be able to work at a steady job which takes her outside of her home. If, however, she is able to bring up her children and care for them herself, I can think of nothing which will probably bring her greater happiness and be more valuable to them, but there are many, many women who do not naturally and happily spend day after day with little children. There is no use in closing your eyes to the fact that women do not become satisfactory nurses and governesses simply because they have brought children into the world.

It may be far better for the children to have a woman actually taking care of them who may never have had a child. There should be between a mother and a child a bond deeper and greater than that which comes in any other relationship and I think that most mothers have a kind of unselfish love which makes them willing to try to understand and help their children, but this does not mean that they are wise disciplinarians or can carry out the proper daily routine to give a child a healthy body and a disciplined character.

XII

VARIOUS OCCUPATIONS FOR WOMEN

WHILE I do not intend to make this a chronicle of all the occupations open to women, I want to mention a few. We can be librarians, secretaries, stenographers, newspaper reporters, photographers, hostesses on planes; in the professions we can be lawyers, doctors, scientists of various kinds; and in the arts women have excelled as sculptors and we have good women poets, writers, painters, playwrights. This list will only serve to fill our pages and not to clarify the purpose of this book, but we may profitably treat a few vocations in detail.

TEACHING

For many years the only occupation which was considered possible outside the home for women was that of teaching. Women became teachers long before they entered any other gainful employment because it was the one occupation which tied in with the life of the home closely and for which it was felt for a long time that very little special preparation was needed. Of late it has become more and more necessary to have specialized training for each subject that one wishes to teach.

One of the great difficulties has been that a great many girls and boys have gone into the teaching profession because they could not think of anything else that they wished to go into. I remember very well going to supper at one of the sororities in one of the larger colleges for women and inquiring what most of the girls were going to do and being placidly told that nine-tenths of them would be teachers, not because of any particular vocation, but because it was the simplest thing to do in the interim before marriage.

Now teaching is entirely different from what it was in the early days and those who undertake it should be very sure that they have a vocation. It is not, however, surprising that girls and boys consider that this profession is one which they can go into with comparatively little real aptitude, because we who constitute the public have given so little thought to what we wish to produce in our teachers and to what we expect from our private and public education. There is a great deal of discussion to-day as to what really constitutes education and many learned books have been written on that subject. There is a fundamental thing, however, that I think every one will accept as being worthy of consideration, namely, no matter what young people study, the important thing is that the study should be vitalized for them by the personality of the teacher. It is far more important for the child to be thrown into contact with some really interesting mind than it is for him to learn a particular group of facts. It is also unquestionably true that some people have an ability to impart information and other people who may be greater students themselves find it impossible to give out what they have stored in their minds, but even this gift of imparting information is not sufficient to make a teacher a great teacher. The quality which makes men or women great teachers is the ability to inspire with curiosity the youthful mind. Different countries have different theories of education. The Germans and the French take their education very seriously and the children must at certain times pass very difficult and complicated examinations which are standardized and presuppose the following of a well-defined curriculum which requires very long hours spent over their lessons every day. Much detailed knowledge is required of children, and particularly in Germany, where it means much to their future life if they fail in passing certain examinations required on the path to successful appointments in government or business positions. For this reason there is a high percentage of child suicides in these countries from sheer discouragement. This is not to my mind a successful result of educational methods.

In England the theory of education is somewhat different. They aim to train the mind, but not to give any specialized vocational training and they have succeeded in turning out a more cultured individual than we do on this side of the water, though our general theory is patterned more on the English than on continental theories.

It is rare to find an Englishman who does not know the classics, because they look upon a knowledge of Greek and Latin as essential to the training of the mind and with the knowledge and appreciation of this must of necessity go the wider knowledge of all the literature which has come down to us. Therefore a greater knowledge of history and a greater knowledge of the countries where this history has taken place is a part of the education of every English child.

It is, of course, easier in Europe where the countries are closer together to have more of an understanding of the history and literature of other nations and also to acquire their languages, but these difficulties will gradually lessen for the people in this country as transportation and communication become easier and our education is certain to go through great changes. The reason that education is becoming increasingly important to us is the fact that we realize we have to decide whether our civilization shall continue to exist or whether it shall decline as have many previous civilizations and something new take its place.

Another war such as the World War would certainly eventually cause the wiping out of our civilization. There is only one way to prevent recurrence of war and that is by better education. Therefore, the reason we are interested in teachers to-day and in our system of education is really because those of us who are thoughtful realize that it has become a question of self-preservation. We can no longer trust the guiding of future generations to young girls or boys who happen to think that they would like to spend three or four years earning a little money in teaching in a school conveniently located near their homes, or, if they do not like their homes, at some distance from them. So this question of being a teacher has assumed much more serious proportions; therefore, preparation for being a teacher must, of necessity, be undertaken not only more seriously by the persons themselves, but more seriously by the community.

I am familiar with a limited number of teachers' colleges and I am convinced that we could greatly improve the training of our teachers and by so doing improve the education of our citizens. In nearly all of our state colleges the youngsters have an opportunity to come in contact with only a few interesting personalities. A good deal is brought to them in the way of lectures or music from outside sources and the rest of their education depends largely on books. When you are young your most vivid impressions come from seeing and experiencing and absorbing new ideas through personal contact. I wish very much that some-day an experiment might be tried, first to improve the teaching of English and then to improve what we call the general background and the wider vision of the teachers.

It is axiomatic that you cannot give what you haven't got and if the amount of education we give our public school teachers is three or four years spent in a normal school or state college not very far away from their homes and then they return to those homes to teach, it is obvious they will take back very little that is new and fresh to the youngsters who study under them.

I would like to see cut to the bone the money spent in mere decoration of school buildings. We want a useful, practical and agreeable interior, an exterior designed with simplicity and beauty. We need gymnasiums and laboratories and schoolrooms with plenty of air and light, but we do not need elaborate carvings and decorated rooms nor marble halls and expensive exteriors. I think also that we waste a good deal of money in the studying of too varied a curriculum. We do need better-paid teachers with the security of a pension at the end of their years of service and above all far better teacher training than we are now giving.

I would like to see some arrangement made by which our young people studying as teachers would agree to spend their years of preparation with only very brief visits home, probably at Easter or in the Christmas holidays each year, and the rest of the time planned in the way some of the big foundations plan their scholarships. The holidays should be given to travel in this country and in Europe so that a teacher going to her work would take back a rich background of things seen and heard beyond the usual experience of the children in her classes. Of course this means that parents must realize that being a teacher requires very special training and that they have to be unselfish enough to give up their children for longer periods every year in order that they may have these opportunities to see more of the world and to be broadened and be able to understand history and literature and human beings in general.

Much more attention and time should be spent on English, and English, of course, includes a knowledge of the literature written in this language.

In this age of specialization account must be taken of any special gifts which a child may have—he must be allowed to specialize along these lines and those who are going to be teachers should develop something which they can do with their hands. More and more we are realizing that it is necessary to develop skill of hand as well as brain and any teacher must be able to understand the value of training in some form of handiwork and she cannot do this unless she has some kind of skill herself.

Hand in hand with all the rest of the teaching course, goes the building of character. No one has more influence in a community than a teacher. These young teachers have the lure of popularity constantly before them and only real character training will make them dominate their young pupils, winning respect, even at the cost at first of easy affection.

I would spend more money than we do now on our teachers' training and I would be extremely careful in choosing the positions in which these young teachers are placed when they first leave college or normal school. They should go under some experienced teacher who will give them their first lessons, not only in the art of teaching but in the art of living in a community, which is always a part of a teacher's job and for which they are usually very little prepared.

I have always felt that in this country where so much depends upon universal education not only for the happiness of the people but for the safety of our form of government, that it was a pity some way had not been devised by which the interest of every one could be focused on public education. I suppose it was thought originally that when everybody had to pay school taxes they would take the necessary interest in public education, but as it has worked out the element in most communities best fitted to choose able teachers and judge what is really worth while in education, is usually considering principally what is happening in the private schools and not giving much thought either to the curriculum or the administration of public education. Perhaps it would not be practical to have everybody send their children to public school because certain children might need different methods in education, but while there are many able people and devoted people who work extremely hard to educate the children of our country, this never makes up for the general interest of all the men and women of a community, and a teacher should enlist and hold their interest.

For our purpose, however, I wish also to bring out the fact that there are new fields opening to women continually besides the old ones which can be handled in new ways, but all of them require certain fundamental qualities in women. Teachers must realize the importance of physical health. They must learn on the whole to keep themselves in good condition and I believe, under the impetus

144

of competition with men, women are developing a stronger physique than our 19th century sisters had. Fundamentally I think women have more strength of a certain kind than men. Perhaps it is better described as a certain kind of vitality which gives them a reserve which at times of absolute necessity they can call upon. They must also learn that no matter how feminine they are, their feelings must not be easily hurt or they will be nuisances in whatever occupations they are working. They must acquire an attitude of integrity toward their work which sets that above all other considerations, except the most vital one of home relationships, and which does not allow them to give less of themselves, even when they themselves are probably the only people who will know whether they have in the language of the school boy "worked up to the limit" or "just got by." They must be generous toward their fellow workers and learn to work with all kinds of people and no matter how critical they may be of themselves, it is well to learn to understand how to handle other people, for many people will do better work when given a little praise than they will for any amount of faultfinding.

All these things we try to teach both boys and girls as part of their education but the circumstances of many

girls' lives do not always make it as easy for them to acquire these qualities.

Year by year, however, what with sports and college
and coeducational courses, girls are finding themselves less
and less handicapped and I believe for that reason that the
day will come when places will be filled by people who are
capable of filling them quite regardless of their sex. This is
the goal for which every woman who is now working
should be striving, for no one wants special privileges
these days, but an equal chance, and for equal work equal
wages should be paid.

If a woman is as well equipped as a man there should
be no question of rejecting her because of her sex. The
teachers of to-day must do the work which will lead to
this attitude in business, in politics and in the professions,
and I think most of us look forward to the day when this
will be the accepted attitude toward women in all the activities of life.

Nursing

One of the other vocations for women which has been a
field open to them from the very beginning is that of

nursing. Nursing in these days has become a very specialized field. There are surgical nurses, obstetrical nurses,
medical nurses, nurses for doctors who specialize in throat
and nose, etc. As the medical profession specialized more
and more, the nurse has specialized in the same way. I
should say in a broad general way that this again is a profession which requires a real vocation. I do not believe
that any one who does not really care about alleviating
the suffering of humanity can become a good nurse. She
must be interested in her patients, or she cannot, with all
the training in the world, give them that sense of personal
devotion which makes a nurse beloved in a household.
They can be the greatest comfort in the world and many a
distraught household have I seen calmed by the presence
of a really good nurse. Then again many a household have
I seen thrown into complete turmoil by the entrance of a
nurse who demanded more than she gave.

In my own experience, I happen to have been very,
very fortunate. In fact, I consider that the very lovely Miss
Spring who came to me when my first baby was born, gave
me in the ensuing years the training which made me able
to cope with the vicissitudes of a large and active family.
She was always a comfort to us all and never a burden; she

was quite willing to go down and prepare her patient's food or her own, if necessary, and there was never any question of having other people relieve her of her burden; she was the one who took on, as far as her duties would allow, the burdens of everybody else in the house.

This is a field in which women who care for this type of work can find utter and complete satisfaction, but it is also a field in which a woman should remember that she will wear out and therefore should make every effort to lay aside a certain amount of money, for her usefulness in her chosen profession will not continue forever.

A regular trained nurse, of course, puts in a good many years of training and in the past there were no regulations as to her hours while on a case. Now I believe these things are better regulated.

Of course, besides private nursing and nursing of private patients in hospitals, there is public health nursing in both city and country. This is social welfare work of a very specialized kind and there are also many other administrative positions—head nurses and their assistants in hospitals, positions in schools, in government buildings and in large business organizations where many employees make it necessary for the management to have a nurse on hand to take care of minor illnesses and accidents in the building, army and navy nurses, and, in addition, there is a big field of missionary work where the practical and tangible side of nursing is often more acceptable than the service of the spiritual preacher and minister, and where the spiritual teaching goes hand in hand with the lessons of health and hygiene.

The cost of a real trained nurse is very high and often not necessary for the patient or beyond the patient's means, and that has led to another occupation—that of practical nursing. For this a woman does not have to have the years of training which lie behind the registered nurse, but she does have to have good common-sense and experience. She has to know how to take a temperature and read a thermometer, how to follow out the doctor's directions and how to recognize the ordinary symptoms of illness.

One of my friends has been a practical nurse for old people requiring companionship and care for a number of years and has, I think, proved that this occupation can be interesting and helpful and carried on successfully by women of mature years. It is particularly satisfactory to find work where the age limit can be extended a little, as one of the most tragic cries to-day is—what can a woman over forty-five do?

Many young girls are also taking a shorter training course and becoming aids to laboratory research workers. They learn to help in the tests and take photographs and do a number of things which are useful to men and women who are carrying out experiments and doing research work along various lines. I think this is only a six months' or a year's course and they are called technicians. This has proved interesting to many young girls and women. All of these occupations provide interesting lives and moderate incomes, but it seems to me that more and more we are coming to realize that people are going to live on more moderate incomes in the future and the important thing in choosing an occupation is to choose something which you enjoy doing so that your reward may not be only in your salary, but may lie also in joy in your work.

In the field of social work, of course there are innumerable varieties of occupations that do nowadays require a course of training and very frequently a college background. But there are women still managing day nurseries and the housekeeping end of settlements who are not college trained and not particularly young. I am stressing this point because so many inquiries come from middle-aged women as to what still lies open to them besides the drudgery of a hotel linen-room or a cleaner's job.

The social welfare worker who makes a name for herself and gets some really important enterprise started has a most interesting life. Women like Jane Addams, Lillian Wald, Mrs. Simkhovitch and Jane Hoey, all of whom have been at the head of some great movement for social welfare, are of course in the very top-notch group, but under them and doing useful pieces of work in smaller fields are innumerable women, women in charge of settlements, women in city departments, women in county work, and each one of them has had the satisfaction of feeling that she has entered into the lives of innumerable families and left them better off than she found them. This must be the compensation for some disagreeable experiences, but I doubt if there are many dull moments for social workers. The problems are always new because human beings are so variable and whether one is working for a church, or an organized association or a branch of the government, the actual daily contacts are with human beings and the variety is endless.

Of course, many of us hope the necessity for much of the work done by social welfare workers will disappear under new ideas of social justice which are gradually becoming prevalent in modern society. All charity should have as its objective not only the immediate alleviation of distress but the future upbuilding of the individual or the family to a point of independence so that charity will be unnecessary.

The civilization of Rome came to an end because individual citizens lost faith in each other, but how can there be any lasting faith between individuals when members of one group are constantly conscious of the fact that their life is so conditioned that they can never hope to leave misery behind them, and attain enduring independence sufficient to provide them with a simple and decent method of livelihood?

Confidence in your fellow citizens can only be maintained in a civilization which makes certain standards of living possible for each and every individual and gives an equal opportunity to every individual to progress as far as his ability and character will permit.

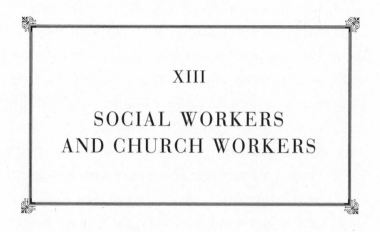

XIII

SOCIAL WORKERS
AND CHURCH WORKERS

THE burden of much of the relief work which is being done
to-day rests upon the church worker and the social worker
in the different communities and therefore I think it is
well to take up these two occupations which are largely
held by women.

I am, of course, very familiar with the work of the dea-
conesses in our own Episcopal Church and while this is
work which requires consecration and great unselfishness
still I think it provides a full and interesting life. Deacon-
esses may be sent to different parts of the country or into

other countries, but wherever they are sent, they find themselves very intimately connected with human lives and human problems. They must, of course, have a desire to be helpful and useful to their brothers and sisters in distress and this same thing holds good of all church workers no matter what the denomination of the church for which they are working. The type of service is exactly the same whether you render it in the New York City slums for the Episcopal Church or for the Jewish Federation, or whether you follow Father Damien in the Pacific Islands caring for the lepers, or work for any other creed. The one real difference which must characterize church workers, however, is the stamp which their own faith makes upon their lives.

I have never felt that missionary work which consisted principally in preaching and in giving out tracts carried very lasting convictions. They must be followed up by living examples. The reason that Christ was such a potent preacher and teacher was because He lived what He preached and the church workers who wish to accomplish the double task not only of alleviating human suffering but of giving faith to the people with whom they come in contact, must show by their own way of living what are the fruits of their faith.

A social worker does not of necessity have to belong to any particular church, but she must have some kind of faith to live by for her life is so filled with the sorrows and hardships of others that without a firm conviction that there is a reason and a meaning lying back of all this, life would become intolerable in spite of the satisfaction of seeing certain accomplishments day by day.

Many of us, of course, believe that charity, meaning the giving of material things, should be taken out of our planned society. We have grown to consider it a charitable deed to give human beings the necessities of life which should be theirs by right and we hope that with a new vision coming to so many, certain kinds of charity may gradually be removed. For the moment, however, there is the necessity for more charity than ever before though it is charity to a great extent given by the government.

The government in its decision to see that none of its citizens shall either starve or go without shelter, has undertaken a colossal "charity" job. But in another sense it is not charity at all because no government or civilization could or should endure which cannot provide people with an opportunity to earn the necessities of life.

It lies very largely in the hands of the social workers to-day to decide how this enormous government responsibility shall be fulfilled. Most of these workers have had imagination and vision and have administered the funds at their disposal wisely and sympathetically, often working against what must have seemed like insuperable difficulties.

One small group of workers whom I have watched recently were, I thought, carrying out the work in a very remarkably efficient and intelligent manner. They were using on relief people who had professions, to carry on their professions for the good of other unemployed, and these people were so enormously interested in their work that they gave not only the time paid for but all of their time in order to alleviate the suffering around them, even though their pay was only relief pay which paid for two or three days a week.

They have so organized the work which they have undertaken that no one in their locality talks about being on relief; they simply talk of doing public work. When the unemployed learn new handicrafts or do some other kind of work besides their regular occupation or the "public" work which has been provided in order to relieve their distress and lack of employment, they are kept from feeling in the indigent class by being allowed to buy the material necessary for the work and paying for it in work, the finished product being sold for that purpose before anything is sold for the benefit of the individual. This way of administering government charity, of course, is far preferable to simply handing out money to buy this or that or to procure things as gifts which might alleviate distress in a household. By making it possible for every individual family to buy at least the minimum required for living, a sense of self-respect and independence still exists in that community.

I have always felt that one of the dangers which is most obvious in the benevolent work taken up by large companies for the benefit of their employees is that it encourages a sense of dependence on the part of the workers. It would be far better if those companies would pay better wages and give their people more time in which to live their own lives outside of the factory or the mill. There is no question that a thing which you establish and work for means more than a thing which is given you. Therefore, if a group of people averaging a decent weekly wage establish a hospital for themselves or a baseball field or a swimming pool, they will feel greater pride and pleasure than they would if it had been presented by the company.

I have in mind a small town I went through once in a southern city. With me in the car was a citizen of that town. We passed a very attractive looking mill. The grounds around were charmingly planted and there was a large baseball field and I had pointed out to me a company hospital, a company nursery for children whose mothers were working in the mill and the company store. Then there were rows and rows of company houses and the whole thing was inclosed by a high wire fence. My neighbor to whom I commented upon the beauty of the plant and the apparent interest taken by the owners in their workmen, replied, "Yes, but we look down upon the mill workers just because they do none of these things for themselves and cannot appreciate them when they are done for them. They came out of the hills and were happier when they were there than they are now entirely cut off from the town and feeling that the people around them are despising them for accepting a miserable wage and letting the owners who will not pay them a reasonable sum for their work, throw them these sops, and keep them in the position of little children to whom the parent says, 'We know best what is good for you; you cannot be allowed to look after yourselves.'"

Paternalism of this kind is not conducive to self-development, neither is it really American.

This is a species of charity which we should wipe out as soon as possible and at present I think we are making an effort to see that decent wages shall be paid for all types of work so that no American need be entirely dependent upon charity for the ordinary necessities of life. However, there will probably be for a long time the necessity for certain types of educational and physical work to continue and that being the case the social worker is the obvious person to carry on this work. When you find a group of social workers doing the kind of work which I have described, it stimulates the ambition and interest of the people so that they will hold a vision before them in the hope of some day achieving it, and here I think the social worker can do her most valuable work for any community. Of course, she has many branches of work open to her. She can work with children, she can work with sick people, as a paid case worker, as a trained nurse, a teacher of almost any craft and as a teacher of almost any type of "book larnin'" as the mountain people would say. She must have an interest in people and a desire to help them, and added to that she must have tact, unselfishness, and a gift for politics, for it is useless to say that she will not often have to be concerned with politics and politicians. A social worker's life brings her into contact with the government of the city, state or nation at almost every step, and the sooner she studies her political situation, the sooner she will be able to understand many of the things which happen and which seem entirely inexplicable. I can think of no occupation which would provide one with more variety and more interest than this occupation dealing with the wrongs and misfortunes of human beings and seeing one's efforts rewarded by better social conditions.

The women of any community, however, are very closely connected with the work of the social worker because I believe that it is part of her skill to interest them and make them social-minded. I have found that in certain communities where a good social worker has lived for a number of years she has completely changed the social outlook of the rich and poor in the community. She has an opportunity of educating people in giving and also in the knowledge of each other's needs. It is really just as necessary for a person who has something to give to find the right outlet, as it is for the person who needs things to find some one to give them, and now that we are seeing the dawn of so many new ways, I would like to emphasize the duty of every woman to familiarize herself with the work of the social workers in her community who are working amongst the less fortunate members of that community. And then I would like to suggest that each and every individual take an interest in his own neighbors. So often in these days we do not know what is happening right next door to us, particularly in the larger cities. If we started with our own immediate neighbors trying to find out what we can do personally for them and did not leave it all to organizations or to professional people, we should gradually find our circle of neighbors spreading.

It seems to me that it is a part of neighborliness not to be interested just in family affairs but to be interested in everything which touches the neighborhood. This is not only a question of giving of money but includes the little things which require individual thought and care. These things which mean the giving of oneself are what make life worth living and educate the giver as well as the one who receives.

Personally I do not hold as very important the amount of money which anybody gives to any charity. Money is a necessary thing to have but the results obtained by spending it are the really important thing. It is very pleasant to have the money to give and that money should be used as wisely and as generously as possible, but real neighborliness is something that could change the whole fabric of our social life to-day.

If you know that the woman next door has a sick child and you have been in to see it, you are not going to rest until that child has every care, any more than you would if it were your own child that was suffering. But if somebody just tells you that Mrs. Smith has a baby with an attack of infantile paralysis you are apt to say, "How very sad for Mrs. Smith," and go gayly on your way.

Close touch is almost necessary for the final little push to personal action, and what could not we do in every community to-day if everybody who has anything beyond her own needs would really take the trouble to be the kind of neighbor the Good Samaritan was. Seeing that this happens is the social worker's real job!

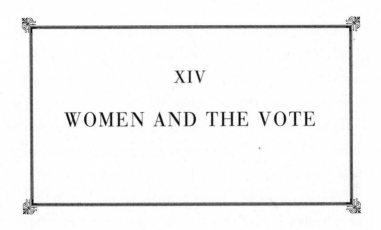

XIV

WOMEN AND THE VOTE

THERE is one new activity which entered the life of women with the passage of the Nineteenth Amendment in 1918. With the right to vote, a whole new field of responsibility and direct power came into the hands of the women of the country. A few of our states had already given women the right to vote and in some communities they were allowed to vote in school elections, but they did not enjoy the full privileges of citizenship as the equals of men throughout the whole country until 1918.

Many fine men and women had worked for this change for many years and the stories of Elizabeth Cady Stanton,

Dr. Anna Shaw, Susan B. Anthony and Carrie Chapman Catt are inspiring reading, because of the unselfish devotion they brought to this cause, which they felt meant a just recognition of the rights of a big group of people. Looking even beyond the justice of the cause they felt this power given to women would herald great changes for the good of mankind.

Fourteen years have now gone by and everywhere people are asking, "What have the women done with the vote?" I often wonder why they don't ask the men the same question, but I realize that it is a high compliment to women that evidently they were expected to bring about some marked change in political conditions and so I would like to look into the question of women as citizens and see just what we have done and are doing and then perhaps dream a little about what we may do in the future.

The vast majority of women, like the vast majority of men, have little time to give to anything but the earning of their daily bread either by actually working themselves or by caring for home and children and making other people's earnings go as far as possible. Their good citizenship consists in leading their lives so as to make them as productive of good for all around them as they can be, and their public duty is expressed by using their vote as intelligently as possible.

A vote is never an intelligent vote when it is cast without knowledge. Just doing what some one else tells you to do without any effort to find out what the facts are for yourself is being a poor citizen. When women first had the vote, many of them did not know how to get information on questions of government. Others had seen the men for years go and vote, had heard them talk a little during the weeks just before election about this or that candidate or this or that party, but had never gathered that there was much concern for the things the parties stood for. You were a democrat or a republican because your family belonged to one or to the other party, because your people had been in the north or in the south at the time of the war between the states, or because it was easier to get advancement in business in your locality if you belonged to one or the other party. These reasons and some others like them did not greatly stir the patriotism of the women. A few women formed the League of Women Voters, a nonpartisan organization which tries, as far as human agencies can do so, to control the prejudices of its members and have them look at both sides of political questions and to furnish unbiased information to any women asking to know about candidates or measures proposed by any political party. Other organizations sprang up for political study and long established women's clubs added departments of citizenship where their politically minded members could study such questions as interested them. The vast majority of women, however, remain as indifferent to the vote and how they use it as are the vast majority of men.

If we look about us in the world to-day or read past history, we will find that benevolent monarchs and good dictators have as a rule had contented, well-governed people. The reason, I fear, is that we are all glad to let some one do our thinking for us as long as we go on fairly comfortably and happily. It is only when bad rulers oppress their people for a long time that those people begin to think for themselves and eventually overthrow their rulers.

Those of us who live in democracies have known of such occurrences in the past but if our leaders have led us through fairly still waters we are as content as other peoples under other forms of government to let some people do our thinking for us, and it takes stern times to shake us out of our apathy.

Women are no different from men in this and though certain subjects may be of greater interest to them, they have been slow as a group to act because political thought and action were new and following women leaders was new. How many times have I heard older women say, "Well, I really feel safer with a man doctor and I take a man's advice on certain questions because he's been at it so much longer than we women!" The sex is still the basis of judgment; they don't just say, "I like Henry as a doctor better than Susie," or "I think James' opinion on that question is more sensible than Jenny's." That day is just beginning to arrive and, strange coincidence, it is arriving just when stern necessity is driving many people in our country to think about questions which for years they have been willing to leave to their leaders.

For a number of years I, with many other women, have traveled our various states trying to arouse women to an interest in government, pointing out how it affected their homes, building and working conditions, the water they drank, the food they ate, their children, the schools, the public health, the recreations. We have used the World War to show how much, as women, we are concerned with governments in other lands and our relations with them. We have showed the necessity for women of different lands, whose fundamental interests are the same, to know and understand each other. We have tried to dramatize some of the lessons learned between 1914 and 1920 as to the waste and futility of war and frequently found a polite response, a temporary burst of interest and then the old apathy creeping back as the sense of present security and comfort spread around our women.

Now, there is for many people no sense of security and no comfort and no ease and no luxury, and even the right to work, not always looked upon as a blessing, has become a precious and sought-after right. Now you do not, either in men or women, have to arouse interest in their government; it is the one hope they have and they look to it for salvation. Political news in papers has become interesting; books on economics and on government are eagerly read; there is a revolution in thinking and that always presages a revolution in action. One can have a bloodless revolution if one can count on leaders of sufficient vision to grasp the goal for which the mass of people is often unconsciously striving, and courage enough in the nation as a whole to accept the necessary changes to achieve the desired ends.

Some women have been educating themselves in the past fourteen years; the mass of their sisters is now awake. Are there women ready to lead in these new paths? Will other women follow them? We do not know, but one thing is sure, the attitude of women toward changes in society is going to determine to a great extent our future in this country. Women in the past have never realized their political strength. Will they wake up to it now? Will they realize that politics in the old sense, a game played for selfish ends by a few politicians, is of no concern any longer to any one and that recognition in the sense of receiving a political job is perhaps necessary but only important because of the opportunity it affords a woman or a man to show what they conceive to be the duty of a government servant? If our government offices are not held in the next few years by men and women with new conceptions of public service, then our revolution may not continue to be bloodless and changes may not come gradually as they are coming now, but violently and suddenly as they have come in the past in France and in Russia and we will go back before we gather up the pieces and move forward again.

So in reviewing the past fourteen years let us acknowledge that women have made a few changes in politics. It is quite safe for them to be at polling places on election day and very gradually the men are accepting them as part of the party machinery and to-day if a woman wants to work and can prove her ability and is not too anxious and insistent upon recognition and tangible reward, she can be part of almost any party activity except the inner circle where the really important decisions in city, county and state politics are made! She can get into this inner circle in national politics more easily than in state, county and city and I wonder if the reason might be that men in Washington are a little more formal with each other and therefore the presence of a woman does not "cramp their style" to the same degree that it would in the other conferences? Women have made no great changes in politics or government and that is all that can be said of the past and now for the present.

Women are thinking and that is the first step toward an increased and more intelligent use of the ballot. Then they will demand of their political parties clear statements of principles and they will scrutinize their party's candidates, watch their records, listen to their promises and expect them to live up to them and to have their party's backing, and occasionally when the need arises, women will reject their party and its candidates. This will not be disloyalty but will show that as members of a party they are loyal first to the fine things for which the party stands and when it rejects those things or forgets the legitimate objects for which political parties exist, then as a party it cannot command the honest loyalty of its members.

Next, I believe women will run for office and accept victory or defeat in a sporting spirit. The proportion of women holding elective office is small. There are two reasons for this: one is that many women have dreaded the give and take of a campaign, they have dreaded the public criticism, they have not learned to discount the attacks of the opposition; but business and professional life is paving the way and this reason will not deter them much longer.

The second reason is that as a rule nominations which are given women by any of the political parties are in districts where it is almost impossible for one holding their political beliefs to win; in other words, a woman who is willing to make a well-nigh hopeless fight is welcomed by a local leader trying to fill out his ticket. The changing attitude toward women in general may bring a change in this. We have good women in political office to-day and much depends on their success. They are blazing the new paths and what is far more important they are exemplifying what we mean by the new type of public servant. When Frances Perkins says, "I can't go away because under the new industrial bill we have a chance to achieve for the workers of this country better conditions for which I have worked all my life," she is not staying because she will gain anything materially, for herself or her friends, but because she sees an opportunity for government to render a permanent service to the general happiness of the working man and woman and their families. This is what we mean as I see it by the "new deal." Look carefully, O people, at the record of some of your public servants in the past few years! Does this attitude strike you as new? If so, the women are in part responsible for it, and I think at present we can count on a more active interest from them and a constantly increasing willingness to bear their proper share of the burdens of government.

Now for the dreams of the future:

If women are really going to awake to their civic duties, if they are going to accept changes in social living and try to make of this country a real democracy, in which the best of opportunity is available to every child and where the compensations of life are not purely material ones, then we may indeed be seeing the realization of a really new deal for the people. If this is to come true, it seems to me that the women have got to learn to work together even before they work with men, and they have got to be realistic in facing the social problems that have to be solved. They cannot accept certain doctrines simply because they sound well. I have often thought that it sounded so well to talk about women being on an equal footing with men and sometimes when I have listened to the arguments of the National Woman's Party and they have complained that they could not compete in the labor market because restrictions were laid upon women's work which were not laid upon men's, I have been almost inclined to agree with them that such restrictions were unjust, until I came to realize that when all is said and done, women *are* different from men. They are equals in many ways, but they cannot refuse to acknowledge their differences. Not to acknowledge them weakens the case. Their physical functions in life are different and perhaps in the same way the contributions which they are to bring to the spiritual side of life are different. It may be that certain questions are waiting to be solved until women can bring their views to bear upon those questions.

173

I have a friend who wrote me the other day saying that because she and her husband lost all of their money, they have been obliged to go and live in a rural community in a small farmhouse. She and her daughters are doing all their own work and they have chosen the community in which they are living not because they found a house which they liked, but because they found a school for the children that they felt would give a real education. After the school was found, they found the house. She adds, "I do not regret the money—it has been a marvelous experience, giving my children a true sense of values, and I have learned what real people my country neighbors are. Because we have struggled together we know each other far better than do the average people who live in far easier circumstances."

There are many people who may make this same discovery and it is not always necessary to lose everything in order to make it, but it is necessary to attain the vision of a new and different life.

I was reading lately a book which Ramsay MacDonald wrote about his wife who died in 1911 and who seems today to be alive as one reads the pages of the book. She was far ahead of her time in many ways, but her most striking characteristic, from youth up, was the feeling of not being able to live in comfort when so many others suffered. She felt that all human beings were her brothers and sisters and her work has lived after her. Many women in this country have been carrying on similar work and perhaps we are going to see evolved in the next few years not only a social order built by the ability and brains of our men, but a social order which also represents the understanding heart of the women.

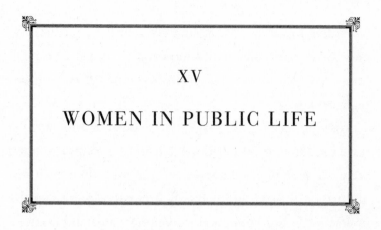

XV

WOMEN IN PUBLIC LIFE

ONE of the questions which I am being constantly asked is, "What openings are there for women in the field of public service?" At the moment there is a clearly awakened interest in this question because for the first time women have been recognized and are holding high offices which bring them before the public eye in government, not only nationally, but in the various states. It has been for a long time customary to have women in the various departments of both national and state governments doing, frequently, expert work as technicians or in positions where study and research work were needed, but as a rule women doing work of this kind get very little recognition and so the fact that many important things have been done by women in public service has escaped recognition by the masses.

Now not only in England, where for some time women have held important positions, but in this country women are placed where the newspapers recognize their positions and this will mean undoubtedly increased interest in the opportunities for public service amongst girls and women.

It seems to me that the first thing is to recognize that any woman who is going to do valuable public service must be very excellent in her job whatever that job may be in the outside world.

Secretary Perkins, for instance, trained herself for years in social work, was interested in conditions of labor and studied particularly the connection between labor and capital for many years before she took a position in the state government. Some women in politics, of course, have not had any training but this is rare and I do not think as advantageous for the women themselves. I think a woman is always more confident of her ability if she feels that she has been trained in work which particularly fits her for the public job which she is undertaking.

Many girls write and ask me how they can go into politics just as a boy might decide that he wished to take up a political career. My answer to the girl is exactly what it would be to the boy—in this country there is no such thing as a public career as such. We must have an occupation in life and take our public service, if it is of a political character, as a side issue, a contribution to our country which may also contribute to our well-being and increased efficiency, but primarily we must consider it as a service to the country. If we look upon it only as a means of earning a livelihood, we will probably be far less useful as public servants.

My experience has been that the men or women who have no other interests but their political positions, do not have very satisfactory lives. Professional politicians in this country mean to most people men and women who serve in the party organizations and usually do not go beyond small local positions.

In England it has always been customary for some people to take up public life as a career, but with us this is not as satisfactory. If one political party is in power, it usually means that most of the people in the opposing political party are without jobs, and therefore they must be able to take up some other work when their party is not in power.

There are, of course, members of state legislatures and judges and congressmen and United States Senators who have such strong holds upon their districts that they are returned time after time regardless of whether the country as a whole changes its political complexion or not. But these are usually men, and sometimes women, who have served their constituents very faithfully and have strong personalities which have so impressed their fellow townsmen that they are able to hold their positions even though new or different ideas may sweep over the country as a whole. The great majority, however, go in and out of office with their parties and therefore, I would advise all young people first to establish themselves in some occupation and then begin by taking an interest in their communities and their local political affairs, gradually working up to other positions in public life. It is very valuable for the young man or the young woman to know from the bottom up how a political organization functions and I personally believe that it is well for all young people to belong to nonpartisan organizations before they join any political party, in order that they may really make a study of the principles for which the various parties stand before affiliating themselves definitely with any one of them. The old idea of a son following in his father's footsteps in deciding on his political affiliations, does not work so well as it used to and daughters, apparently, are even less inclined to follow in the family footsteps. Youth is more individualistic than ever, it seems, and desires to make up its own mind as to what political party it wishes to join and regardless of the prejudices of their elders, many young people insist on deciding for themselves where they wish to throw their weight. I think girls are even more independent than boys in this matter because they have less opportunity for discussion at home or abroad and their political interests come as entirely new fields to them.

If they are going to be really active in politics, it is just as well for girls and women to start doing things in their own communities, such as helping the associate county chairwoman bring people in on election day to the polls; acting as tellers or watchers until they finally can take some position, such as member of the county committee or state committee.

The basis of all useful political activity is an interest in human beings and social conditions, and a knowledge of human nature.

This is not something which can be acquired overnight and that is why I suggest that young people—particularly young women—come to their political activities from the bottom rather than from the top. If they come from the bottom, there will undoubtedly be times when they will feel that political life is sordid, that human beings are disappointing, that their aspirations and desires are frequently rather low, and it is just as well to realize all this, for no useful work is accomplished until facts are faced and accepted. If you are going to be discouraged by finding that people do not always measure up to what you expect of them and by finding out that everybody does not always believe in the old adage that "honesty is the best policy," the sooner you get over that discouragement the better. It is well to remember the old fable of the tortoise and the hare. Pegging along day by day, is a dull way of changing the world and it is far more exciting to be Garibaldi, but probably it is the plodders who in the long run accomplish the most.

When a woman has mastered the details of party organization and has gained a certain amount of knowledge of her fellow human beings, then she may be ready to accept either an appointive or an elective office. She will be far more effective because of this service in her party organizations.

Every few days somebody writes and asks me whether I think we will some day have a woman President of the United States and I am afraid that I look upon this question with a certain amount of amusement, for it is really unimportant of what sex a President may be. We certainly will not have a woman President until some woman worthy of being President appears on the horizon. In the meantime, men both worthy and unworthy will probably fill that office. In the course of human events it may come to pass that we shall only consider an individual's qualifications and the sex will pass unnoticed, but that is some years away and in the interim, I do not advise any woman to try to be President, or in fact to hold any important office until she has gained experience in minor offices first and feels herself capable of filling easily whatever office she is striving for. During the next few years, at least, every woman in public office will be watched far more carefully than a man holding a similar position, and she will be acting as a pioneer preparing the way for many other women who will follow in her footsteps.

Public office, however, does not mean that one goes in only for positions which are affected by political organizations. There are certain services where technical knowledge is necessary and it is quite possible for a woman to fit herself to enter one of these services. Many women have done so and are at present serving as research workers and technical workers in many government offices regardless of what political party may be in power.

They are also going in to-day for the diplomatic and consular services. To do this they have to pass the regular examinations and get an appointment to some foreign post. Once in, however, they progress in the same way as any other employee in the service. No one goes into either service with any idea of remaining permanently unless they take the examinations. People frequently write me and want temporary appointments because they speak a certain language and are visiting the country where that language is spoken or because they want some experience abroad. The only way in which a temporary appointment of this sort can be secured is through personal acquaintance with some one at the Embassy who is willing to take one on, if one is willing to render free services for the experience one may get, and services are needed in a temporary clerical job; but one cannot be a paid government servant. Candidates are not taken on by the government without passing examinations except in the cases of certain clerks and minor employees and these are not considered as part of the regular Government Foreign Service and are not actually diplomatic or consular agents.

To me one of the most necessary things for any one who wishes to go into this particular branch of the government's service, is a gift for languages. I do not believe it is possible unless you speak the language of a country really to understand the people themselves and, after all, the fundamental thing which our consular and diplomatic agents must do is to understand the people with whom they are maintaining contact. A diplomatic agent must represent his own country but he must be able to appreciate also what is good in the country where he is living in order to represent his own country sympathetically. He must have interest enough to study the history of that country, its literature, and try to work out a way by which he can make his country understandable to the people of whatever country he may be in. It is not always the heads of missions—the ambassadors or the ministers—who do the most important work in drawing nations together. It is often the consuls in small towns and the assistants who do more to build up the good feeling and to promote international understanding than the head people could ever do because they cannot come in such close contact with many people in the community in which they are living.

Many young men have made starts in their careers as lawyers through having served a year as secretary to one of the Justices of the Supreme Court. Justice Holmes for years made it a practice to take students from the Harvard Law School who had graduated with high honors, for the first year after they left law school and I think that none of the young men who served under him fail to look back upon that year with gratitude for what they learned, and with deep affection for their chief who did much for them in many ways besides giving them their first legal experience.

These services are not strictly speaking political services but they are public services and prepare men and women to earn their livings in the outside world as well as in public service.

It may be that the time will come when boys and girls may definitely plan to enter public life and to make their living by doing so, but at the present time I think this is out of the question. The fear of being thrown out of a job unless he is sure of being able to find something to do, or has already made his place where he can easily return, is bound to affect the usefulness of the public servant. He or she is bound to act with an eye to reëlection or reappointment and the most useful public servant is the one who can freely make up his mind as to what is the right thing to do and act without any regard to his own future, politically speaking. This may mean temporary eclipse, but in the end I feel very sure that it is the wise thing to do from the standpoint of a political career as well as from the standpoint of the good of the State.

A man or woman in public life must learn to listen to everybody's opinions. They must never be prejudiced or dogmatic, they must keep an open mind, but when they have listened and know what they think themselves, they must have the courage to stand by that. They will frequently be accused while they are listening, of vacillation and weakness, but this will do them no harm and it is far better than being obstinate or trying to act without the full knowledge of the situation and the benefit of as many points of view as possible. But, having once made up their minds, as to what they believe and what they are going to do, it will win them real friends and the respect of their constituents and co-workers if they stick to the objectives that they wish to accomplish.

Courage and a realization that a public servant has an interest in the community which is greater than his interest in himself, will in the end, I think, win recognition and approval from a constituency whether it be large or small. There is no question but that the most important work in a democracy is that rendered by the servants of the people.

XVI

WOMEN AND
BUSINESS TRAINING

In the letters which come to me one subject is constantly being forced on my attention, namely, that many women grow up with little or no knowledge of business, and are therefore an easy prey for people who are dishonest and are simply trying to make money easily without any regard for those from whom they acquire it. These absolutely dishonest promoters of dishonest schemes are not the only people, however, who may injure unsuspecting and inexperienced women. There are dreamers in business who are quite sure that their schemes are going to succeed and bring fortunes to every one involved. They are not dishonest, they are simply visionary, and the persons who are taken in have no case against them because they themselves should have had enough sense to know whether the scheme suggested had a chance of being successful.

I believe very firmly that every child should be given some business education besides the ordinary standards of honesty. They should be taught that you do not spend money until you have it, that money represents somebody's work or the production of some material things for which some human beings in some way have worked. Money is only a token but it is a token which represents real things; therefore, if they expect to acquire it, it is only fair that they should give something in exchange. Real work of some kind must attend the honest making of money. A child should be taught that certain things are worth saving for and that one way of making money is to save it. But the really important thing for every one to learn is that plausible people who tell you that by doing nothing you can make a great deal of money, are not telling you the truth. I had a letter a few days ago from a woman who asked if I would ask my husband to tell the people whether he intended to keep up the stock market prices or to let them seek their own level, as it was very hard on the investor not to know what was going to happen! Now, the obvious answer to this plea is that the lady is not asking information for a bona fide investment group, but for a gambling group. She tells of a working woman who took her savings and bought fifty shares of a certain stock.

It is very unwise for any one to take all of his savings and buy one stock which he knows nothing about, particularly on margin as this woman must have done. Any wise business investor when he is not using money which he can afford to risk, investigates the business in which he wishes to invest, and buys outright an interest in that business either through the purchase of stock or bonds, but he does not buy on margin. If this stock fluctuates a few points it will mean little to him because as long as the business is on a sound basis, he will get his interest.

There have been serious wrongs done to many unsuspecting people in this country by urging them to invest in things which sound safe and which are very unsafe. I personally do not think that a small investor who can not get the best of business advice, should have anything to do with the stock market. One of the causes of the most spectacular and extremely disastrous periods in the finances of this country was the fact that too many inexperienced investors were in the market.

I think as a whole it is better for us not to try to make fortunes overnight, but to be content to live within our means, to save for an emergency and for the future and to take care of our money in a conservative way with the exception of that part of it which we may decide we are willing to risk and lose if necessary for the fun of gambling now and then.

The spirit of gambling seems to be in all people. We may regret it, we may legislate against it, but in one way or another, the gambling spirit seems to spring up again—on the race course, in the stock market, in the lotteries which are so popular in European countries or in card games in the drawing-room and crap games in the street. Therefore, it seems impossible to say to people—you shall not gamble, but at least you can suggest that the part of the wise man is to gamble only with that which he can afford to lose. Even the wisest of business men are finding that in times such as we have been going through their money has been invested in things which are going down. No one can be sure that what they do is safe, but government bonds as long as the government keeps within its income and does not borrow too heavily, are good investments even for the small investor if he is willing to accept modest interest return on the capital investment. Postal savings banks, in fact all savings banks in ordinary times where the banks are of good reputation, are safe custodians of the people's savings with very modest returns in the way of interest.

The great majority of people, however, in this country are earning only just enough to save toward buying a home, and perhaps having a little something put aside for the education of their children and for their old age. The average careful person carries some kind of insurance for sickness and death, for even being buried costs money!

There are forms of short term insurance which if taken out with reputable firms are safe investments for people of moderate means and one can put in one's money knowing that one will be able to get it back with interest or in the form of an annuity at the end of five years or ten years or whatever the term may be.

The first principle, however, which we must all learn and keep to, is that whether our incomes are large or small, whether they are in the form of salaries or interest on invested capital, whether they are earned with our hands or with our heads, we must try not to spend more than we actually have on hand. I sometimes think this principle is harder for young people to live up to than for older people because so many things are greater temptations to them. A girl likes pretty clothes, a man has his own peculiar extravagances and I think perhaps the best thing we can do for our children is to teach them to be able to pass by something which they want and forget about it afterwards. I know a young lady who may not buy the dress she wants but when she hasn't bought it, she will talk about it so constantly that her husband in the end, if he can scrape together the money, will go and buy it for her and she will then accept it as though the money had dropped from the sky, when as a matter of fact that money should have been saved toward a rainy day.

These times have taught many of us the wisdom of foresight and self-denial, but when things are over they are soon forgotten unless the educators of the country realize the necessity of impressing upon children for the future some of the lessons learned through the hardships of the present.

XVII

WOMEN AND WORKING
CONDITIONS

THIS is a time when working conditions for both men and women are undergoing very violent changes. It has usually been an accepted fact that women should be paid less than men. The original theory on which this idea was based, I imagine, was that men were physically stronger than women, could work more hours and do heavier work. But since machinery has so largely come to be the order of the day, this has changed. Women in factories and in shops find themselves quite able to do the same work that a man does if they go into the work at all. This being the case, it would seem advisable that the principle of equal pay for equal work should be accepted, otherwise employers who wish to keep down the cost of production will largely employ women and pay them less than they would have to pay men. It would be natural to wonder why women are willing to work for less than men. There are a number of reasons and perhaps the main one is that women employed in industry generally do not expect to work all their lives, but look forward to the day when they will be married, and therefore are not so deeply concerned with wages or working conditions outside their own homes. This is all very well and for the unscrupulous employer very satisfactory, but it is not good for labor in general, not good for men who work and not good for women who may have to continue to work throughout their entire lives.

Great efforts have been made to make working women realize the necessity for union organizations but very little result in the way of actual organizations can be seen. Now and then you will find women are organized in some trade, but it is very apt to be a trade where they are allowed to enter the same union with the men and where the men's union had already been established.

One would think that enough women of intelligence would have recognized this problem and educated the great body of working women. This, however, does not seem to be the case and women in industry continue, largely because of their own lack of initiative, to receive lower wages than men and to pull down the wage scale of the men as well as their own.

In occupations where the higher type of women with a better education is employed, they are more nearly getting to an equality and I think before many years in the professions and the more skilled trades and more executive jobs, we shall see very little difference in the earning capacity of women as compared with men. Women should receive equal pay for equal work and they should also work the same hours and insist on the same good working conditions and the same rights of representation that the men have. If they accept longer hours and unsanitary working conditions, they injure the cause of labor. This may mean, however, if they are not allowed to join the men's unions, the forming of a union of their own, but I hope it will not be as difficult in the future as it has been in the past to awaken them to the necessity of organization. I think women have a right to demand equality as far as possible but I think they should still have the protection of special legislation regarding certain special conditions of their work and until we actually have equal pay and are assured of a living wage for both men's and women's work, I believe in minimum wage boards and regulating by law the number of hours women may work. They should also be allowed a certain number of days off before and after the birth of a child. This legislation is primarily necessary because as yet women are not as well organized or as able to negotiate for themselves with the employers, but it is also necessary in the interests of the state, which must concern itself with the health of the women because the future of the race depends upon their ability to produce healthy children. The new codes aim to accomplish many of these things, but the codes must be enforced and public opinion must insist on this.

There is one type of occupation in which women are largely employed which is entirely unregulated. In the old days there were in this country comparatively few domestic servants and there are still only a small number of households where the home maker has any paid assistants, but in every community there are some households where this is necessary. I remember reading in some early history of American homes that the lady of the house would take in one or two of her friends' daughters and teach them how to do certain things in the household. They were her maids but they were also her friends. In one case which I remember the lady of the house did all the mending not only for her own family, but for her maids as well! That was the day when domestic service had not sunk to the lowly place which it now occupies in the scale of employment. I believe that domestic service of some kind is going to come up again in the world as an occupation for women, but I also believe that house-holders are going to change their point of view regarding servants. This is easier to do in small households where only a mother's helper or at most two maids are em-ployed, where the owner of the house and the maids are working together and nobody feels that it is beneath her to perform any household tasks. In larger households this question of domestic service becomes more complicated and I think that we are going to find ourselves obliged to make domestic service a real business occupation. We have seen in New York an experiment where maids were trained and went out on an eight-hour-day basis, taking their food with them and performing certain tasks in the household but neither sleeping nor eating there.

Some people found this a very admirable arrangement, others complained bitterly that it was not feasible and special difficulties were found where children were concerned. I think it may be difficult to achieve a complete standard of hours in a household where nurses or governesses form part of the establishment because they are more nearly on the basis of executives and are always allowed to work as many hours as is considered necessary. They have the interest of the position itself at heart as the executive has the interests of the business as a whole in his mind, and are not concerned only with the wage scale and how many hours are necessary to earn a stated sum of money. A mother, a nurse or a governess is in this category where children are concerned, but they should have fixed times for recreation when they are free from responsibility, for they need it even more than any other members of a household. The rest of the business of running a house can and should be organized on a regular business basis and the sooner we accept this necessity the sooner will some of our employment problems come to an end. A new occupation will be open to some of our older people who will be retiring from industry and many of our households will find their burdens immeasurably lightened.

I hope that the maid of all work, household drudge, will never be allowed again. She had no hours and her wages were low; but she was usually a foreigner and, with restricted immigration, she has, I think, disappeared, as she undoubtedly should.

The stigma once removed from domestic service, intelligent and ambitious young people will be ready to enter this service as well as the older people who, as I have suggested, may find here a partial solution to their employment difficulties. I feel that the modern woman should take a particular interest in the conditions under which all women are going to work because the basis of much of our present-day unrest is the discontent of the working class generally with the returns which they receive for their labor. If we women who are usually the ones most concerned in keeping peace, whether it is peace between nations or peace between the employer or employee, do not concern ourselves with working conditions as they affect the social conditions of our day, then we can hardly expect that any advance toward a satisfactory solution of these problems will be made in the future.

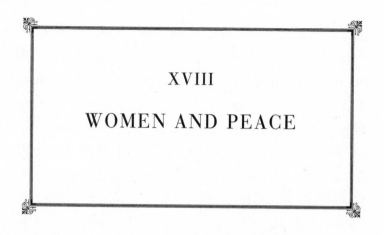

XVIII

WOMEN AND PEACE

ONE of the things in which women are vitally interested to-day is the abolition of war as a means of settling disputes between nations, and I feel that this is particularly a question which is up to the women. Over and over again have I sat and listened to men talking since the close of the World War, and almost invariably they will voice the sentiment that it would be a fine thing if we never again needed to resort to war, but that human nature is so made that men will always feel that they must fight. This seems to be the instinctive reaction of most men. I find amongst many of the men who actually fought in the last war a very distinct feeling of the futility and waste and a real horror of the cruelty and filth, coupled sometimes with a firm decision that nothing will again drag them into the trenches of modern warfare. In the younger generation, however, there is still a lure in the martial music and flags flying and the mere adventure which any great risk holds for youth. The explanation, of course, is that when you are young, the blood courses hotly through your veins and though you may face the fact that death may be imminent at any moment, you never really believe it. The process of slow detachment from life has not yet begun and that is why there will always be young men ready to fill up the ranks of the fighting forces of war.

As I see it there are two things which women must do. One is to create a *will to peace* in all things and the other is to make adventurous some other things in life besides war. The *will to peace* will have to start with women and they will have to want peace sufficiently to be crusaders on the subject.

Joan of Arc, who was only a simple peasant girl, had a vision of how she could lead her country through victorious war to freedom. The women of to-day must have a vision of how to lead the world to peace. Those of us who remember the World War, who are old enough to realize how it came about and then to see something of the results in human suffering, remember many of the catch words with which youth went to the slaughter. It was a "war to end war," a "war to preserve democracy" and here fifteen years later in the Far East the yellow races are fighting each other, the Navy of the United States is on the Pacific Coast, we are building more ships, not because we want to fight, but because we are afraid not to live up to our neighbor's strength.

Europe is alive with rumors of war and there has been blood shed for one reason or another in many places. The world is apparently sitting constantly on high explosives and cannot be changed. When advocates of war want to be more scientific they say it is one way for removing from the face of the earth the surplus population. Well, I can think of more humane ways of doing this if the theory is true. I much prefer to choose my own way of leaving this world to having it chosen for me by some foreign nation's machines of war.

We are also told that all of life is based in nature on the principle of constant struggle and survival of the fittest. But the world is evolving new ideas and we find that the policy of a free-for-all struggle such as was the rule in the past, is no longer as satisfactory as it used to be even in business, and perhaps we are going to find that this is true all along the line. In any case it can never be said that war is an act of God. Famines may be; a pestilence which comes about through no fault of human beings may be—though we have learned little by little that ingenuity and greater scientific knowledge can conquer a good many of what were considered in the past acts of God—but war is always the act of men.

I think, though, before we eliminate wars between nations we probably will have to learn to eliminate the desire that individuals have to force other individuals through physical violence to do their will. There are ways to bring about acceptance of the decision of the majority of society that certain acts are unsocial, and they need not involve physical violence. If we learn to apply these methods in our personal contacts and in the discords which arise between different elements of society, we may also learn to use the same methods between nations.

Force is probably never a safe weapon to use and our ingenuity may have to be bent to discover other safer ways of teaching individuals and nations that they must abide by the accepted rules of society as a whole. The first thing to learn is that freedom must always be qualified by the fact that your own freedom must not mean somebody else's slavery.

Thought is a very great influence in the world and if all the women can get together and agree that differences of nationalities, differences of customs must exist, but that the time has come when quarrels of whatever nature shall be referred to courts of law, this will be done. We accept the decisions of courts in the punishment of crimes of violence, and in practically all the civilized countries in the world there still are times when the passions of human beings get the better of them and individuals fight each other. Sometimes they murder each other, and yet we believe in the court system and its success. There might still arise cases when some individual nations might so completely forget themselves as to ignore the existence of a court, but some machinery can surely be devised which could handle this emergency—either an international police force or an agreement by which the other nations would isolate those nations, cutting off their necessary supplies or in some way making life for them so difficult that they would soon come to their senses.

If we really acquire this *will to peace*, we will gradually impart it to our children, but we will have to give them something to take the place of the adventure and excitement of war. We will have to go even further and devise something to take the place of the sacrifice which is so great an element in patriotism and which no matter how selfish youth may be, is the element in their nature which drives them to deeds of heroism and to heights of unselfish devotion which they would be incapable of except in times when they feel the call to be somewhat greater than they really are.

In the past this same spirit has been called forth by devotion to the church, devotion to the king, devotion to some causes. We see the same thing in the youth of Russia to-day; they are casting aside religion to substitute a new one under the name of communism. We see it in the youth that follow Mussolini and Hitler. There is a chance that we may see it flower in America through devotion to a real democracy and the revival of a religion which shall not be a doctrine nor a theory, but a way of life.

I heard some one say the other day that until now he had never really been interested in America, but for the first time his own country had become a vitally interesting and important thing because it was possible to see developing new social ideas that would allow all human beings to have a certain amount of happiness and the opportunity to develop what was best in them.

I have been in many different types of homes lately, some of which could hardly be termed homes, being nothing more than shelters where people who were almost animals were living. They slept on the floor on filthy sacking; they carried whatever water they used from quite a distance, so washing was not a common habit. Their food was anything found on the floor or on the table or out on the ground which would fill up empty stomachs.

A child had a rabbit as a pet, and an older child said rather mockingly as the small boy brought out his pet to show me, "He says he won't let us kill it to eat when it grows up, but we will see about that." At these words the hunted-looking little boy grabbed up his pet and fled— one touch of humanity in what was scarcely a human household.

And yet in another community where living conditions were not exactly ideal either, a woman made a scrapbook of pictures cut out of any magazines she could lay her hands on and she called it her "house of dreams."

It was the story of what she would like to have as a home and of what she would like this home to mean to her children. If you can live in such surroundings and still have such aspirations, then there is something for the youth of the nation to be unselfish about, something for the youth of the nation to find worth while making sacrifices to attain. We must have the *will to peace* in our various countries, between the people who have had material things of life in great abundance in the past and those who have had little but grinding toil. Then when we achieve this kind of peace there will be fewer incentives which will drive nations to war with each other. We will have less greed because there is less to covet of our neighbor's goods.

Then youth must realize that this new freedom, which sets new value on human endeavors, makes it more important to work at something one cares about and to do it well than to make large sums of money at anything else. It offers to all of youth a challenge to organize this new world, and to right the wrongs that exist without creating new wrongs, for sometimes when we correct one wrong, we bring about another.

This challenge to organize a new social order not in one place, but all over the world, has possibilities of adventure and excitement, a society which of itself should take the place of the old glamour surrounding war. Only the women and the youth of any country can initiate this change. They will have the men to help them later on in the fight, but they will meet some of the same unbelief and lethargy that they have come up against in the past. A crusade with recruits such as can be found to-day, persistently carried on, will, I believe, establish a *will to peace* and a new conception of how to live, which will mean victory for future generations. Eventually we shall have a real international court and a real league of nations and a real plan for handling those that every now and then may be recalcitrant.

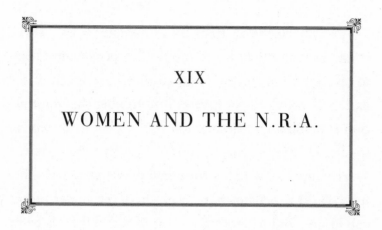

XIX

WOMEN AND THE N.R.A.

OVER and over again it is said that women are the buyers of the country. The National Recovery Act is an act to enlist the services of the manufacturers and the distributors of all types of merchandise, as well as the public represented by the ordinary citizen. All these ordinary citizens are the buyers and consumers of the country.

It is up to the women to organize their households and themselves, to see that they live within their incomes, that they buy as fairly as possible from the fair merchants and buy only such goods as are manufactured by fair manufacturers.

It is not always easy to do this. Information as to who is fair and who is not is difficult to get, but people must learn to take a little more trouble than they have taken in the past, and with comparatively little trouble this information is obtainable whether you buy at chain stores or in the little corner grocery or in the large department stores. You can find out whether the employer is fair and whether the goods he deals in have been produced under proper conditions, and whether the spirit of the N.R.A. is being lived up to by that company.

The general purpose of the codes is to help in the revival of business and at the same time to establish a fair treatment of employees. They aim also to establish a just and reasonable return to the employers and stockholders of a company. This is not just an emergency measure. It is hoped that out of all the negotiations, a permanent basis of fair play to all will be established and by watching now, the women will help to lay this permanent foundation.

In a number of industries the heads of the industry under these codes have had it intimated to them that they will not be able in the future to receive as large a salary or enjoy as many bonuses as they have in the past.

These things are all more or less familiar and comparatively well understood. What we are principally interested in as women is our place as consumers. In the days of speculation one great evil crept into the consumers' lives, namely, the evil of installment buying far beyond the proper sum which should be spent in this way. Of course, it is extremely laudable to want to own a home and a very wise ambition, but in the past, perhaps a man would have saved 20 per cent of the cost of the home which he needed. Why not instead of taking such a big mortgage and placing such a tremendous burden of debt upon one's home, wait until one has saved at least 40 per cent of what one is going to spend? It would mean less risk of the loss if hard times come before final ownership is established. One of the most pathetic things which have happened in the last few years is that people have seen swept away from them all the money which they have put into small homes in prosperous times because the burden of carrying the interest on the mortgage was too great. In the same way when you are buying anything on the installment plan, it would be well to consider carefully what percentage of your income you can afford to pay out for what you are buying. I remember well hearing about some neighbors on one occasion who had to pay 48 per cent of their income for very delightful possessions, such as the electric ice box, the sewing machine, the radio, etc., when it would have been better to wait for any or all of these things until there was no question of saddling themselves with such a burden of debt, for the remaining 52 per cent of their income was not sufficient to live on satisfactorily. Some emergency may arise—sickness or a new baby or an unexpected catastrophe—and if you have mortgaged yourself in this way you will rue the day, for you may lose everything which you have made partial payments on because for a time you cannot keep those payments up.

Under the N.R.A. the slogan should be "Deal with fair people and make sure that they are fair with their employees and to their stockholders; spend what you can but spend it wisely and do not mortgage your future!"

Hoarding money because you are afraid of what may happen will be the means of bringing about the very results you fear. You can very easily figure this out for yourself in your own community. If you do not go to the nearby store and buy your customary amount of merchandise, you will suddenly find your neighbor doing the same thing and the demand for what you have to sell if you sell in your own neighborhood will be less and less. This is no time for the hoarding of money simply because we are afraid that the country is going to the dogs. If it does, our money will do us no good so we might as well spend what we can wisely. As a matter of fact, if we stop spending we are taking a course which will inevitably lead to the very brink of disaster again. Save what you must save for old age or education or sickness, but put it where it will be of use to some one and it will return to you perhaps enhanced slightly in value. A savings bank or a wise investment is a good way to provide for emergencies in the future. Don't keep your money in a stocking!

We women in the home have another great responsibility. We have allowed certain practices which are wrong to grow up among the business men of the country. Had we always insisted that the men take into account the human element that entered into business there would not be the fight there is to-day over what is the fair standard of living for every one in this country. Had we said we will have none of your products which are produced without consideration of these standards which we believe in, somehow or other by now it would all have been changed.

Of necessity a good deal is being changed now, and it will change more rapidly if some of us who have made the discovery that we can help to bring about these new standards will offer our services to try through our lectures or our writings to tell others how they can help in this campaign for a fairer industrial organization.

This country was founded on the theory that we must work together and help each other, and that each man or woman's problems affected the whole community. We all remember reading of the husking and quilting parties when all the neighbors joined together and worked for each other and had fun doing it. We remember the tales of our grandfathers working together building stone fences and clearing fields and raising houses and barns, all of them cooperative undertakings. As we have grown in size and in wealth we have drifted away from the community help-each-other spirit and the belief has grown up that each entity is independent of any other and sufficient unto itself. The past years of depression have shown us that we cannot live for ourselves alone—and it is the women fundamentally who can reëstablish the old idea which worked so well in laying the firm foundation of our country. Women can begin now to inculcate it in their children whether they live in cities or small communities. They will be surprised to find that it will bring them not only greater security but a greater happiness and content which is bound to be the result of unselfish thinking and doing.

This is a time which should teach us all one lesson—namely, that the prosperity of the few is very precarious indeed if the many are in really poor circumstances, and so whether we are rich or poor we have a very strong interest in the success of the present National Recovery Act. If we are economically independent and can give our time to doing something toward awakening the interest of other people so that each individual will do his share, we need not limit ourselves to the broad principles which I have laid down. We can and should offer our services to the administration itself; we can go out into the country as speakers; we can see to it that in the community in which we live no injustices are allowed to stand without rectification.

No chain is stronger than its weakest link and it is well for the women, if they have independent means, to realize that the time has come when drones are no longer tolerated. If a woman is not busy with the necessary duties of life, such as the care of her home and of her children, a care which requires her physical presence and physical work, then she must be ready to do something else in this emergency or in any other emergency which may arise.

I have made the suggestion that women join with the N.R.A. administration and go out as speakers, that they see that information which will help them as consumers is made available and I have also suggested that they organize themselves and their households.

I know a woman who has one maid in her house but that maid is on an eight-hour schedule not because her mistress is so absolutely convinced that she should have time off, but because her mistress has decided that she wants the best possible service and she cannot get it if her maid is worn out by long hours and little opportunity for rest or recreation.

You can readily see that not only is this maid a better maid but on the whole she is a better citizen. She has the leisure to read and be informed, besides time for recreation.

If every woman would organize herself and think of those around her as carefully as this woman has, we would soon find that our chain was a very strong one and that our women were doing their part intelligently and humanely.

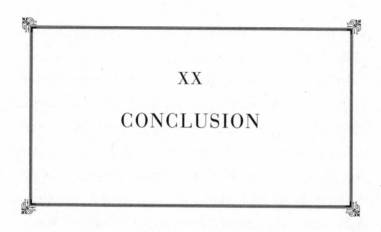

XX

CONCLUSION

THE subject matter which I have treated in the foregoing chapters has been covered before in many articles and speeches which I have written and given, and I am not vain enough to suppose that many other people have not covered it far better than I have. But in the course of a varied life, I have found that some things may be treated in many different ways and that what will appeal to one person may not appeal to another. There is no harm in reading a variety of points of view. It accomplishes one very desirable thing. It sets us thinking even if we differ with the writer so that we eventually discover what we really think ourselves.

In the foregoing chapters I have touched on the things which to me are the most important in the necessary adjustments which we must all make to life to-day. Our relationship to our family and to our homes! In spite of everything, it is the homes of America which still form the basis of our civilization. We older people may have to make some adjustments to meet the different ideas and the different conditions facing the younger generation but if families keep their love and affection for each other, and will try to be tolerant and understanding of each other's problems, in the end I think our civilization will not suffer.

I have taken up the subject of women's work in the business and professional field and because this is, comparatively speaking, new, there are constantly new problems arising in connection with it. But they are solving themselves little by little and I think the position of women and their usefulness is increasing constantly.

And last but not least, through it all I have tried to give an idea of what I feel to be our obligations as women to the new social order which is growing up about us.

I am no philosopher. I cannot lay claim to more than the usual ordinary individual's education or culture but I have had opportunities for mixing with a great many people in a great many parts of the world and no one can do this without being forced to think out a certain philosophy of living. In these chapters I hope I may have given the interest to other women to think out for themselves the things they wish to achieve as the result of our civilization in this country. What kind of world do they wish to leave behind as an inheritance to their children? It does not matter much whether we leave individually money or worldly goods of any kind, but it matters a great deal where we throw our weight in the development of society.

To illustrate this, I should like to tell you the story of a woman whom I know well. She is comfortably off, but one day she said to me, "I try as far as possible never to invest in any business which is not run according to the principles which I believe in. Of course, it is impossible to acquaint oneself with every business but one can usually tell sooner or later something about the greater industries and I will not share in any money which has been made by keeping down wages or by giving poor working conditions." She added, "I do not believe in prohibition but even when it is legal I would not want any stock in any company making or selling hard liquor, for I believe that it has a detrimental effect upon our citizens and I will not make any money out of human weaknesses."

If every one of us in our business transactions could have as high standards of ethics as has this woman, I think a good many of our difficulties between labor and capital would be ironed out without any strikes. But too many of us in the past have thought first of the material gain and the fact that we wanted to leave our children safely provided for. That is impossible. The only safety that any individual has is his own character and you cannot make any one person's future secure unless you secure the future of all.

It is important that women think beyond the mere moment through which we are passing and acquaint themselves with all phases of life and conditions in our own country. I think we shall have fulfilled our mission well if when our time comes to give up active work in the world we can say we never saw a wrong without trying to right it; we never intentionally left unhappiness where a little effort would have turned it into happiness, and we were more critical of ourselves than we were of others.

When I was a little girl, my grandmother would often say to me, "You are a girl and I expect you to be more sensible and more thoughtful than your brothers." She was of the generation which did not demand so much recognition for women, but which accomplished many things by working through the men when they hardly knew they were being influenced. I do not mean for a minute that we should go back to the ideas of that generation or that women should return to the old status. I am merely pointing out that women, whether subtly or vociferously, have always been a tremendous power in the destiny of the world and with so many of them now holding important positions and receiving recognition and earning the respect of the men as well as the members of their own sex, it seems more than ever that in this crisis, "It's Up to the Women!"

FURTHER READING

Jill Lepore

The best and most comprehensive biographical treatment is Blanche Wiesen Cook's three-volume study, *Eleanor Roosevelt* (New York: Viking, 1992–2016). A valuable account of her marriage is Joseph Lash, *Eleanor and Franklin* (New York: W. W. Norton & Company, 2014). A recent collection of Roosevelt's autobiographical writings is Eleanor Roosevelt, *The Autobiography of Eleanor Roosevelt* (New York: HarperCollins, 2014). A further source of her many forms of communicating with the public is Stephen Drury Smith (ed.), *The First Lady of Radio: Eleanor Roosevelt's Historic Broadcasts* (New York: The New Press, 2014).

Eleanor Roosevelt (1884–1962) was an American politician, diplomat, and activist. She was the longest-serving first lady of the United States, holding the post from March 1933 to April 1945. She made Gallup's list of "People that Americans Most Widely Admired in the 20th Century," and *Time*'s "The 25 Most Powerful Women of the Past Century."

The Nation Institute

NATION
BOOKS

Founded in 2000, **Nation Books** has become a leading voice in American independent publishing. The imprint's mission is to tell stories that inform and empower just as they inspire or entertain readers. We publish award-winning and bestselling journalists, thought leaders, whistle-blowers, and truthtellers, and we are also committed to seeking out a new generation of emerging writers, particularly voices from under-represented communities and writers from diverse backgrounds. As a publisher with a focused list, we work closely with all our authors to ensure that their books have broad and lasting impact. With each of our books we aim to constructively affect and amplify cultural and political discourse and to engender positive social change.

Nation Books is a project of The Nation Institute, a nonprofit media center established to extend the reach of democratic ideals and strengthen the independent press. The Nation Institute is home to a dynamic range of programs: the award-winning Investigative Fund, which supports groundbreaking investigative journalism; the widely read and syndicated website TomDispatch; journalism fellowships that support and cultivate over twenty-five emerging and high-profile reporters each year; and the Victor S. Navasky Internship Program.

For more information on Nation Books and The Nation Institute, please visit:

www.nationbooks.org
www.nationinstitute.org
www.facebook.com/nationbooks.ny
Twitter: @nationbooks